1994

Still Crazy After All Thes

This book is about women moving, by direction or indirection, by their own volition or by others' representations, on the street and on the page. The starting point is a question of rhetoric – as much in the writing of feminism as in other writings about women. How do texts construct possibilities and limits, openings and impasses, which set the terms for the ways in which we think about what a woman is, or where women might be going, whether individually or collectively?

First, two literary women, Virginia Woolf and Jean Rhys, explore the possibilities for women to walk or write in ways that diverge from those laid out for them on masculine premises, in literary streets already well-trodden by men. Feminist theory – from Betty Friedan to the journal *m/f*, and the continuing Anglo-American fascination with French feminism – then landscapes the discursive territory in unpredictable ways. The last two chapters, meanwhile, return to Freud and the implications of his 'crazy' situating of femininity, as a non-existent place.

Bowlby's work – readable, playful, and pointed – will appeal to anyone interested in feminism, women's writing, consumer culture and psychoanalysis.

Rachel Bowlby is the author of *Just Looking* (1985) on consumer culture, literature and femininity, and *Virginia Woolf: Feminist Destinations* (1988). She is a Reader in English at Sussex University.

Still Crazy After All These Years

Women, Writing and Psychoanalysis

RACHEL BOWLBY

ROUTLEDGE

London and New York

First published 1992
by Routledge
11 New Fetter Lane, London EC4P 4EE

Simultaneously published in the USA and Canada
by Routledge
a division of Routledge, Chapman and Hall, Inc.
29 West 35th Street, New York, NY 10001

Set in 10/12pt Palatino by Witwell Ltd, Southport
Printed and bound in Great Britain by T J Press Ltd, Padstow,
Cornwall

British Library Cataloguing in Publication Data
Bowlby, Rachel
Still Crazy After All These Years
1. Title
305.4

Library of Congress Cataloging in Publication Data
also available

ISBN 0-415-08639-6
      0-415-08640-x (pbk)

Contents

151, 273

Acknowledgements

Different versions of chapter 1, 'Walking, women and writing' appeared in *Tropismes* 5, (1991) and in Isobel Armstrong (ed.), *New Feminist Discourses* (Routledge, 1992). A shorter version of chapter 3, 'p/s', appeared in *m/f: The Woman in Question*, ed. Parveen Adams and Elizabeth Cowie (Verso, 1990). Chapter 4, 'The problem with no name', first appeared in *Feminist Review* 27, (Autumn 1987); chapter 5, 'Soft sell', in *Women: A Cultural Review*, vol. 1, 1 (April 1990); chapter 6, 'Flight reservations', in *Oxford Literary Review*, vol. 10 (1988); chapter 7, 'The judgement of Paris', in *New Formations* 9 (1989); and chapter 8, 'Still crazy after all these years', in Teresa Brennan (ed.), *Between Feminism and Psychoanalysis* (Routledge, 1989). The author is grateful for permission, where required, to reprint.

More personal thanks to the friends and colleagues who contributed to the writing of these essays recapitulate those to be found in *Shopping with Freud*, which appears shortly after this book.

Introduction
The woman in the street

This book is about women moving, by direction and indirection, by their own volition or by others' representations, on the street and on the page. It is about motions for change, movements that disturb. Like *Shopping with Freud*, the companion volume to this one, it brings together feminism, psychoanalysis, consumerism and literature. Here, however, the starting point (there is no conclusive end to the trip) has to do with a question of feminist rhetoric. How do women write what they want (and what they don't want)? And how do the texts written about them construct possibilities and limits, openings and impasses, which set the terms for the ways in which we think about what a woman is, or where women might be going, whether individually or collectively?

For the woman in the street is no neutral opposite or complementary number to that figure for sociological averageness, the man in the street. First of all, the woman occupying this place – in the phrase, on the road – reveals the bias of 'the man in the street' who was supposed to stand or speak for men and women at once. The second point follows from this: that the woman in the street is somehow out of place, at least out of *her* place, viewed primarily in terms of her sex – in the same way that the 'streetwalker', openly sexual, is always assumed to be female, despite the neutrality of the word. In this context, feminism might be looked upon as women's attempt to move themselves into this place on other terms – whether to claim the right of an equal access, or to change the aspect of a scene in which their differences have been disregarded, devalued, or only imagined from masculine points of view.

The first section of the book is concerned with the woman in the street as a walker – a female counterpart to the male *flâneur*, or (and the two are far from being mutually exclusive) the *passante* or passing woman of a modernist literary tradition, glimpsed by the *flâneur* who sees her as the one and only just at the point when she is already out of sight forever. A chapter on Baudelaire, Proust and Woolf (with a perverse beginning in Plato), and another on Jean Rhys's novel *Good Morning, Midnight* develop these scenes in their relation to questions of subjectivity, consumption, and the possibilities for women to walk or write in ways that diverge from those laid out for them on masculine premises, in literary streets already well-trodden by men. The woman in the street is not the equivalent of the man in the street, that figure of normal representativeness; and her sexually dubious associations give to her stepping out a quality of automatic transgressiveness that is also the chance of her going somewhere different. In Woolf, this is a matter of hope; in Rhys, there is a melancholic stasis to the possibilities which the narrator imagines for herself, which appears to prevent her from moving at all.

One of the questions raised by considering how the urban women of Rhys or Woolf might differ or depart from those of Baudelaire or Proust has to do with how lines of progression are set up in feminist argument such that something must be seen as surpassed or superseded in order that forward movement may be seen to have taken place. 'p/s' develops the related example of how to think about the place of a feminist journal in the context of a history of feminist theory and writing. Written on the occasion of the publication of *The Woman in Question* (1990), an anthology of articles from *m/f*, the piece explores the dislocations of perspective involved in a journal returning to view some years after ceasing publication. This is the paradoxical story of the *passante* who does come back, like a ghost from the past, into a present in which she is bound to look older, because things have moved on, while it is also partly through her own influence from the time of her first appearance that they have. The 'p/s' is not just a postscript; it also refers to a particular distinction between the psychic and the social which, in retrospect – looking back now, from this second *m/f* moment – can be seen to have acquired a structuring importance in the way that the forms and styles of feminist arguments were developed in the journal. For the complex 'psychic' questions of female subjectivity, the special language of French theory was brought in, while for those deemed to be the purely 'social' issues – from legal rights to crèches for babies – a more ordinary language was considered to be appropriate.

The chapters in the middle part of the book continue this exploration of the relation of new and old movements in feminism to the forms of feminist writing. Betty Friedan's *The Feminine Mystique* (1963) traced the problem of American middle-class women's identity in the early sixties to the insidious influences of advertising, but doubled the difficulty by making the counter-case in terms uncomfortably close to the forms of persuasion that it was denouncing. Friedan's idiosyncratic version of feminist history – freedom won and then voluntarily abandoned – also raises questions about the implied psychology of women (or men), in relation to both the sources of a sense of female oppression, and the conditions of feminist argument in relation to other forms of persuasion, such as advertising.

Friedan's book, which deals explicitly with relations between consumption and femininity, suggests how these issues are in turn connected to questions of female subjectivity. And it turns out that this is true the other way round as well: the language of marketing may also emerge unexpectedly in the context of debates about subjectivity and social forms which seem to have nothing to do with it. The following chapter, 'Soft sell', looks at how consumerist models of thinking can surface unintentionally, as though by nature, in feminist theory whose aim is in fact to demonstrate how discourses come to seem natural rather than social.

The next two chapters look at further aspects of the rhetoric of feminist criticism. 'Flight reservations' and 'The judgement of Paris' consider an opposition that was becoming standardised by the mid-1980s, between (sophisticated) French and (naively simple-minded) Anglo-American approaches to thinking in feminist and literary theory. This involves rhetorical moves similar to, and overlapping with, those operating when consumption is being used as the simple, negative term against which to measure the complexity of something else. These chapters are also concerned with the way in which such differences are played out across a distinctively postmodern scene: in place of the questionable woman walking in the city, we now have the feminist telling the stories of her flights between Paris and other less marked destinations.

The final two chapters move on, or back, to one of the bastions or bugbears of feminist argument: the debate about feminism and psychoanalysis (though here too there are some interesting globetrotting adventures identifiable along the theoretical route). 'Still crazy after all these years' follows the argument through in all its impasses, both within the history of the debate and in the stumbling blocks and sticking points of Freud's own writing, where there is simply no place for the girl to go. But the last piece, on Freud's study of Jensen's *Gradiva*, sees something different (though no less equivocal and uncertain in its future directions). Here is a Freud text about a figure who is an interesting kind of *passante* – the girl next door appearing as an enigmatically anonymous ghost – but which also gives to the woman the power to move the plot on. Out of her implicit critique of the rigid categories associated with a masculine way of thinking, Gradiva comes forward as a woman who can take herself, and the possible futures of feminist thought, somewhere else, as she steps in on the established patterns of thinking with the assurance of her irony: playing for a change, and playing in all seriousness.

Chapter 1

Walking, women and writing
Virginia Woolf as flâneuse

PRE-AMBLE

Since this chapter is about walking, it seems reasonable to start out with a footnote. This will be covered, later on, by a bootnote. A footnote should be at the end; this one, right at the start, takes us back, to Plato's *Symposium*, to the speech of Aristophanes in that text, and its recounting of an unfinished history of walking – in fact of the prehistory of walking, a sort of pre-walk, rewalked or reworked, which will be my pre-amble.[1] *The Symposium* is anyway constructed around a walk (the narrator got it from his friend as they strolled into Athens); and this walk partly involves the recounting of another walk (at the beginning, Socrates goes with his companion to a drinking party). Aristophanes' tale is about the pre-walk and pre-women (and pre-men, too) that make their later variants look strange, make the image of normality (upright men and women) seem deviant, a humorous wrong turning, in relation to the beings from which they originated.

Plato's Aristophanes tells the story of how humans were first of all divided into three, not two sexes: the male, the female and the male-female, known as the androgyne or hermaphrodite. From the later perspective, these are all double: they have two heads facing outwards, two arms, two legs, and so on. Punishing them for aiming too high and trying to climb up to heaven (ambition is the first urge), Zeus has them all cut in half: the all-males divide into two males, the all-females into two females and the androgyne into male and female. Having lost their other half, literally, all these creatures long to be reunited with it. This is the origin of desire, as a wish to restore an earlier state of things. It is also the origin of male and female homosexuality (the desires of the halves of all-males and the halves of all-females) and of heterosexuality (the desire of each half of the former male-female, the andryogyne).

In the twentieth century, in the context of the widespread and newly 'scientific' interest in questions of sexual tendencies and the differences of the sexes, this part of *The Symposium* has been a constant source of fascination; and in particular, it offers a myth of the equal naturalness of homosexual and heterosexual tendencies – or at least for none being more natural than the others. Freud alludes to the story several times – in the context of the death drive (the wish to restore an earlier state) and also in relation to sexuality. In the *Three Essays on the Theory of Sexuality*, he uses it when introducing to his readers the idea that not all sexual desire is between the two sexes:

> The popular view of the sexual instinct is beautifully reflected in the poetic fable which tells how the original human beings were cut up into two halves – man and woman – and how these are always striving to unite again in love. It comes as a great surprise therefore to learn that there are men whose sexual object is a man and not a woman, and women whose sexual object is a woman and not a man.[2]

But what comes as an even greater surprise here is that Freud has misremembered the myth to which he is referring. He takes it as solidly heterosexual, in order to reinforce the norm he is going to surprise his readers by disturbing; whereas in fact the existence of homosexuality, of what the next sentence calls – in inverted commas – 'inversion', is exactly what Aristophanes' story would lead us to assume.

This misremembering of Plato – Freud lights on exactly the right spot to prove his point but inverts its significance – is surprisingly common. Freud forgets the homosexual pairs all the better to produce them as a scandalous novelty; other readers develop an opposite tendency, remembering only the naturalisation of homosexuality and omitting the heterosexual member of the trio, equally natural in the myth of origin. Sometimes, the hybrid hermaphrodite alone is remembered, but taken as an image of original perversity, whereas it is in fact this creature, who looks most monstrous to modern eyes, which is the origin of the norm, male and female heterosexuality. And it follows from this too that far from being paragons of polymorphousness or promiscuity, as they are often seen, the post-hermaphrodites, and the other two kinds as well, are probably the most unswervingly monogamous creatures that ever walked the earth: they all want nothing better and nothing more than to rejoin forever their one and only lost other half.

But to use the terms heterosexual and homosexual is already to distort again. For in a sense, all three sexual types are both homosexual and heterosexual. They all seek to reunite with someone of the same sex (man to man from the all-male, woman to woman from the all-woman, man to woman from the hermaphrodite). And they all seek to form a couple: the 'hetero-' preposition has nothing to do with male and female, but simply means 'the other of two'. These disorientations of view then suggest some further speculations about the categorical blinkers through which we tend to talk about homosexuality, as about men and women. Freud is not yet using the terms 'homosexual' and 'heterosexual' when he writes the *Three Essays* in 1905; later on, he does. The words are new constructions of his time, consciously formed from Greek roots as so many scientific terms were at the time. Freud does not see male and female homosexuality as parallel formations united in the same difference from heterosexuality. But yoking the two forms of homosexuality under the same word, as our language now does, reinforces a dual opposition between heterosexuality and homosexuality; and it fixes the perspective in advance in implying that they have more in common with each other than they do with heterosexuality.

Later, as I said, these three inconceivable figures may return to haunt us or kick us in a bootnote, in the form of some other odd trios which disturb the securely dual vision of the difference between the sexes and their respective orientations. For now, though, it is time to move forward to a later, more familiar episode in the history of walking and sexuality.

THE *FLÂNEUR*

I am going to talk about walking and this chapter, perhaps inevitably, will be a bit of a ramble. I shall be focusing for much of the time on writing by Woolf, after first looking at some texts by Baudelaire, Proust and a lesser-known French writer. The title 'Walking, women and writing' is not only meant to allude to the questions Woolf raises all the time, in her novels and in her essays, about the relations between women and writing, art and sex, fiction and femininity, and to the way in which she has been taken up as a key source for enlightenment on such issues; it is also intended to recall the expression 'wine, women and song'. Not to suggest that the pleasures of wine are replaced for Woolf by the perhaps less obvious pleasures of the obligatory constitutional: after all, it is she who, in *A Room of One's Own*, having experienced the differences in dining facilities between two 'Oxbridge' colleges, one for each sex, demands 'Why did men drink wine and women water?',[3] suggesting the benefits of wine for inspiration. Instead, the change of words is supposed to evoke the way in which Woolf puts in question the traditional status of women as at once the inspiration of literature and its object: as represented, but not themselves writers.

In thinking about women's writing, there is a tension which comes back again and again between on the one hand narratives of straightforward advance, whereby modern women are taken to be slowly putting past restrictions behind them, getting to stand on their own two feet and write what they want; and on the other the description of formal structures of exclusion, whereby what does not go along with a norm defined as masculine is taken as disruptive of established spaces and in a certain sense feminine. The distinction is between access to something regarded as neutral, and subversion of something defined as normative and masculine. This tension is explored throughout Woolf's own writing about women's writing. Sometimes, she talks of 'impediments' – literally what stands in the way of the feet – obstacles without which women would be able to move on. And sometimes, she talks of the outsider's place, the position of exclusion, as the origin of a difference of view which is valuable precisely in that it does not fit in with and thereby challenges the standard. Following this line, certain or not, we could simplify the two alternatives as between two sorts of walk or step – progressive, or the forward step in a given direction; and transgressive, or the walk that crosses and challenges set lines of demarcation, a step from or to a place represented as beyond the pale, out of bounds.

Let us start, however, from the male walker or writer from whom the woman has to take one of her leads, whether to follow him or to throw him off course. The figure of the *flâneur* epitomises a distinctive nineteenth-century conception of the writer as walker, a sort of man about town with ample leisure and money to roam the city and look about him. Women are not *flâneuses* in the nineteenth century, and for reasons that are not only sociological. A popular text by Louis Huart entitled *Le Flâneur*, dating from 1850 and illustrated among others by Daumier, may provide some indications on this point.

Huart sets up his definition of the *flâneur* largely by way of descriptions of those who pretend to, but do not deserve, the designation. One such case is the *musard*, whose English equivalent would have to be the loiterer on street corners. The *musard*'s fault is that he wastes his time, for instance by stopping in front of just one shop without even being capable of choosing the best one. Another of these pseudo-*flâneurs* is the *badaud étranger*, already a fully fledged specimen of the assiduous modern tourist:

> Le badaud étranger consomme tout à son aise les innombrables curiosités du lieu [le Jardin des Plantes]. Il compte avec soin tous les cailloux de la galerie minéralogique, toutes les herbes plus ou moins exotiques du cabinet d'histoire naturelle, il calcule combien on pourrait faire de boutons de chemise avec les défenses de l'éléphant . . .
> Le badaud étranger s'est dit, le matin, en se levant: – Aujourd'hui je verrai onze monuments! – Pourvu que le soir en additionnant il trouve bien le compte de ses onze monuments, il pense qu'il n'a pas perdu sa journée et il s'endort avec une conscience aussi satisfaite que celle de *Titus* lui-même.
> A peine arrivé devant son monument, le badaud étranger prend à peine le temps de lever les yeux sur les colonnes ou autres accessoires, attendu que sur les cinq minutes octroyées à ce dit monument, il en accorde quatre à la lecture de la description qui en est faite dans le *Guide du Voyageur*.[5]

Neither too much nor too little attention to places, then, is required in order to qualify. But the *via media* in relation to locus and focus is not enough to characterise the genuine *flâneur*. Let us say straightaway that one of the criteria which exclude you is the fact of being accompanied by a woman. There is first of all Sunday *flânerie*, with the family, 'où l'on prouve que le flâneur est un mortel essentiellement vertueux'.[6] But the monotony of closed shops, 'une série ininterrompue de volets verts' (Ch. IV),[7] bears no comparison with the more serious risks on other days of the week, which are firmly underlined by Huart:

> Des flâneries faites en compagnie d'une femme sont encore plus à éviter.
> – Comment! même avec une jolie femme, me dites-vous.
> – Oui, monsieur; et surtout avec une jolie femme!
> Car les femmes ne comprennent les flâneries et les stations que devant les chapeaux des marchands de mode et les bonnets des lingères, – à moins pourtant que ce ne soit devant les cachemires et autres bagatelles, dont l'aspect seul donne le frisson à tout mari, ou à tout autre Français exerçant un emploi à peu près analogue.
> Quand on conduit sa femme ou sa maîtresse aux Tuileries ou au spectacle, ce qu'il y a de plus économique, c'est de prendre une voiture.
> Le malheureux qui veut faire cette économie de trente-six sous court risque de payer en place un chapeau de trente-deux francs, – ou de passer pour un avare, ou pour un être masculin peu galant.
>
> (Ch. XV)[8]

So women are disqualified from *flânerie*, a uniquely masculine privilege, for pragmatic reasons: you, the man, have the money which she, the woman, is going to want to make you lose.

But the woman is also, more tellingly, excluded a priori. For *flânerie* involved a certain conception of the woman as being herself part of the spectacle, one of the curiosities in which the *flâneur* will want to take an interest in the course of his walking. Huart has much to say on this; it seems clear from the outset that the woman is essential to the *flâneur* as an object of his wandering gaze:

> Parlez-moi des Tuileries et des Champs-Elysées! Voilà des lieux de promenades où l'on trouve du moins tout ce qui fait

le charme des flâneurs, - nous voulons dire des femmes, des arbres, des enfants, de la foule, et Polichinelle!

(Ch. XIV)[9]

Further, the woman you see is potentially to be pursued - and this is one reason why you should never *flâner* with a friend:

Vous voudriez suivre une simple grisette, pendant que votre coflâneur vous ferait écraser, ou, pis que cela, éclabousser par la voiture d'une grande dame qu'il aurait voulu admirer de trop près.[10]

But you have to be sure of keeping your distance, not going all the way. You do pursue, but the woman must remain separated from you:

Nous pardonnons l'affection pour la marchande de modes, tous les goûts sont dans la nature, mais nous pensons qu'il ne faut pas pousser cette affection jusqu'au fanatisme. . . . Le flâneur a donc parfaitement le droit de suivre de l'oeil la jeune modiste qui, sous le nom de *Trottin*, va porter à domicile de charmants petits chapeaux et des amours de petites capotes; mais il faut toujours y mettre de la réserve et de la discrétion.

(Ch. XI)[11]

Follow with the eye, not with the foot: that is the recommendation; and there are even advantages to be gained from showing oneself in this respect different from others:

N'imitez pas ces grossiers personnages qui suivent les femmes d'une manière effrontée; une pareille conduite est justiciable de toutes les bottes vraiment frrrrançaises. - Au lieu de marcher sur les talons de la vertu, établissez-vous le défenseur, le protecteur de cette même vertu effrayée, qui vient se réfugier auprès de vous, comme une pauvre colombe palpitante, pour échapper aux poursuites de ces hommes ignobles qui insultent toutes les femmes.

(Ch. XI)[12]

The moral is thus: don't pursue, and the woman will come after you herself.

Before leaving Huart's *flâneur* who, as we have seen, prefers to be left on his own, let us just note two more points. First, the woman – the object *par excellence* of the *flâneur's* interest – is in this regard analogous to the shop window. Huart conludes with another series of exclusions:

> Ne flâne pas ou ne sait pas flâner celui qui marche vite, – celui qui baîlle dans la rue, – celui qui passe devant une jolie femme sans la regarder, devant un étalage ou près d'un saltimbanque sans s'arrêter. Le vrai flâneur a droit d'ignorer le grec, le latin, les mathématiques, et les autres superfluités scientifiques; mais il doit connaître toutes les rues, toutes les boutiques de Paris, savoir au juste quelle est la plus jolie chapelière, modiste, charcutière, limonadière. Il doit savoir par coeur toutes les affiches de la capitale.
>
> (Ch. XV)[13]

It is also notable that *flânerie* goes together with literature: 'Le flâneur compose tout un roman, rien que sur la simple rencontre en omnibus d'une petite dame au voile baissé' (Ch. VIII). The walker is a writer; and what he notes, with his eyes and with his pen, is the woman. This woman cornered by pen or eye does not, at first sight, look like someone likely to take herself for either a *flâneur* or a writer. If she tried to *flâner* or to write, she might be obliged to identify herself as a man, or at least not to look like a woman. This is the predicament of all the female Georges and others of the nineteenth century. Further along, however, we shall see some possible alterations in the perspective. For Virginia Woolf, it is less a question of (masculine) walking as writing than a completely different turn: she tends to think of writing itself as like walking. But this is to get ahead of ourselves: we have other leads to follow before we get to Woolf.

A *PASSANTE*

The place of the walker as writer is marked out from the start as a masculine identity which locates women as part of the representation. Before thinking of or passing to other possibilities, let us cast a glance at her whose generic name takes in all those dress-shop and hat-shop assistants and others who are part of the feminine scene which is viewed or consumed by Huart's *flâneur*. Baudelaire's poem 'A une passante', 'To a passing woman', which was written not long after Huart's text, is perhaps the classical evocation of this figure:

> La rue assourdissante autour de moi hurlait.
> Longue, mince, en grand deuil, douleur majestueuse,
> Une femme passa, d'une main fastueuse
> Soulevant, balançant le feston et l'ourlet;
>
> Agile et noble, avec sa jambe de statue.
> Moi, je buvais, crispé comme un extravagant,
> Dans son oeil, ciel livide où germe l'ouragan,
> La douceur qui fascine et le plaisir qui tue.
>
> Un éclair . . . puis la nuit! – Fugitive beauté
> Dont le regard m'a fait soudainement renaître,
> Ne te verrai-je plus que dans l'éternité?
>
> Ailleurs, bien loin d'ici! trop tard! *jamais*, peut-être!
> Car j'ignore où tu fuis, tu ne sais où je vais,
> O toi que j'eusse aimée, ô toi qui le savais![14]

Amid the clatter and din of the street, there she is; or there she was, no sooner there than gone, vanishing, disappearing, here only in what is now the loss of her. But the poem brings her back: gone/here, *fort/da*, brings her back fixed and no longer fleeing, but fixed as one who flees, 'fugitive', runaway, 'tu fuis'.

He looked, she looked; I looked, you looked; there was an instant, it could have been for ever, it is past.

You knew, 'toi qui le savais', you didn't say. Silent woman who knows, whom he sees knowing, who will not or cannot say.

He looks at her, she looks at him. Two looks, his at her and hers at him? Two looks fusing into one? Or two looks, different? Or one look, his that sees her seeing him (seeing her (seeing him))?

She brought new life ('m'a fait soudainement renaître'), and is also a murderer ('le plaisir qui tue') coming in funeral garments, who fled away free ('Fugitive beauté', 'tu fuis'). In mourning, she has lost someone; she transmits her loss to him, leaving him marked by her passing. Death-dealer and life-giver, a mother.

A twofold mother. 'Moi, je buvais', 'I was drinking', in her eye, nourishing eye and evil eye, 'la douceur qui fascine et le plaisir qui tue'.

Anonymous: any woman, 'une femme'. And also the one and only, the unique woman, love eternal, at first and last sight.[15]

Two women seen in one. She is 'noble', 'majestueuse', a queen or goddess with her statuesque leg; unavailable, inaccessible, she is not to be approached. At the same time the woman of the street, the street-walker. A fast ('fugitive') lady. The whore, undomesticated, whose home is the *maison de passe*, the street inside.

From the third person, 'une femme', to the second, 'toi', addressed at the end: 'ô toi que j'eusse aimée!', you whom I would have loved, past unfulfilled conditional – if what? No answer, she disappeared, never to return, consecrated in the restoration of the imaginary moment when it might have been that she was there. Unconditional love: under no conditions could it be, its possibility is past, ruled out, from the start; and also without interference from external conditions of space and time, in eternity.

The timing puts her definitively in the past, bygone, as the one who passed, irrevocably, and yet will have marked him for ever. She is out of time, no sooner here than gone, represented only in her absence. And out of time because only 'in eternity', in the timeless, will he see her again. There was a flash of light, 'un éclair', then darkness, 'puis la nuit'. The snapshot of what looked like a woman, caught, taken, in an instant, remaining only in an image, the picture of her.

In the distance between them, only their eyes 'meet': otherwise they are apart. He is fixed, transfixed ('crispé'); it is she who moves, 'passa' across the field of his vision. On this separation between them, in space as in time, depends her perfection, and the unconditional quality of the love.

THE *PASSANTE*

But we have not seen the last of this *passante*, a *passante*. She turns up again, and repeatedly, in Proust's vast novel. Here is one such occasion:

> Les charmes de la passante sont généralement en relation directe avec la rapidité du passage. Pour peu que la nuit tombe et que la voiture aille vite, à la campagne, dans une

ville, il n'y a pas un torse féminin, mutilé comme un marbre antique par la vitesse qui nous entraîne et le crépuscule qui la noie, qui ne tire sur notre coeur, à chaque coin de route, au fond de chaque boutique, les flèches de la Beauté, de la Beauté dont on serait parfois tenté de se demander si elle est en ce monde autre chose que la partie de complément qu'ajoute à une passante fragmentaire et fugitive notre imagination surexcitée par le regret.[16]

Proust's *passante* might be a direct descendant of Baudelaire's. 'Fugitive' once more, she is the fleeting impression, only there in the moment that she is already gone. She is statuesque, 'comme un marbre antique', both noble and dead, her own monument, like the 'jambe de statue' of the sonnet. But the 'mutilated', 'fragmentary' nature of Proust's *passante* also, now, looking back, seems to have been shared by that 'statuesque leg', just one leg, one part, singled out by Baudelaire. And the 'regret' here is like that inferred from the poet's 'ô toi que j'eusse aimée', her loss the condition for the desire of her, and for the conditional being necessarily in the odd time of the 'past unfulfilled'.

The *passante* here seems to have moved on or away from her Baudelairean singularity, fixed now into a type: not '*une*', but '*la*' passante. There is not even a question, this time, of a look in return, from her. 'Fugitive' still, her fleeting appearance is not because she passes – she may be quite stationary, in the back of a shop – but because he does – or because 'we' do, a community of (masculine) readers invoked for the occasion as sharing in, recognising, this as a commonplace experience, and the appeal to whom is a further reinforcement of the generalisation of the scene. And if we ignore generic differences between lyric poetry and narrative prose, we could note that whereas the poem, in its title and in the concluding apostrophe ('ô toi . . . ') is addressed to a particular *passante*, Proust's narrator addresses 'us' who are not *passantes* but viewers of *passantes*, on the subject of *passantes*, a general category. The generality of the experience, recognised as an example of a common type, removes its apparent uniqueness and irrevocability: one *passante* is like another in that she can be replaced, that another and another will figure in the same way, without there being any single, constitutive event, even in retrospect.

Putting the two together, Proust's spectator appears to extend and confirm what was only potentially there in the Baudelaire poem. Quite explicitly, the *passante* is now in every sense a mere projection from the spectator.[17] Her passing is really his, as he zooms by just catching sight of her; her partial and fleeting appearance belongs to the same phenomenon. Whence the hypothesis that Beauty might just be 'the complementary part added to a fragmentary and fugitive *passante* by our overexcited imagination'. The 'Beauty' is not out there, but born of 'our' own 'imagination surexcitée'; it is *added* as the missing, 'complementary' part to make a whole of what would otherwise be just the fragmentary vision. It is this addition, carried over to her from us, which completes her, raising her up to the heights of a capitalised essence. 'La Beauté' substantialises her fragmentariness and puts a stop to her disappearance, her passing ('fugitive'). It fits her to him, makes her in the image of his 'imagination surexcitée' prompted by her loss, 'le regret'.

Let us note, before leaving Proust's multiple *passantes*, that the mutation of this figure into pure projection, pure fantasy, may well mark an important turning point in the unpredictable passage of or to women walking and writing. One moment in the course of *A la recherche du temps perdu* brings this sharply into focus. It is the single occasion on which the narrator makes the mistake of actually pursuing a passing woman:

> Je n'ai jamais rencontré dans la vie de filles aussi désirables que les jours où j'étais avec quelque grave personne que malgré les mille prétextes que j'inventais, je ne pouvais quitter: quelques années après celle où j'allais pour la première fois à Balbec, faisant à Paris une course en voiture avec un ami de mon père et ayant aperçu une femme qui marchait vite dans la nuit, je pensai qu'il était déraisonnable de perdre pour une raison de convenances, ma part de bonheur dans la seule vie qu'il y ait sans doute, et sautant à terre sans m'excuser, je me mis à la recherche de l'inconnue, la perdis au carrefour de deux rues, la retrouvai dans une troisième, et me trouvai enfin, tout essoufflé, sous un réverbère, en face de la vieille Mme Verdurin que j'évitais partout et qui surprise et heureuse s'écria: 'Oh! comme c'est aimable d'avoir couru pour me dire bonjour!'[18]

Neither beautiful, young nor anonymous, Mme Verdurin is the antithesis of every defining characteristic of the *passante*, quashing the enigma with the brutality of her all too familiar familiarity. Given that so many mistakes can be made which, in the normal course of things – when the narrator has the sense to keep his *passante* at an imaginary distance – go unnoticed and have no effect, we might consider dropping the only remaining attribute which links the actual and the imaginary *passante* here. For Mme Verdurin, whatever else she lacks or possesses, is, after all, still apparently a woman. But Proust could have gone even further. For if the *passante* is merely or mostly the man's projection, a creature of the masculine imagination, then the field, or rather the street, might be thought to have been left wide open for women to come along and walk in a way of their own – or for quite different, unrecognisable kinds of passer-by to appear.

WOOLF'S *PASSANTE*

Woolf's work contains extended explorations of the relations between women, walking and writing; so much, sometimes, does it appear that the three are natural companions for her that it can seem as though the figure of the masculine *flâneur* had been pushed off satirically down a cul-de-sac, as someone from whom the adventuring woman had nothing at all to fear (still less to desire), on the streets or on the page. Yet the Woolfian street is not empty of men, of their way of representing women or a woman's of seeing herself as represented by them.

Such an encounter is wittily enacted by a section from *Mrs Dalloway*. Peter Walsh, who has left Clarissa's house until the evening party, finds his attention diverted by a classical *passante*:

> But she's extraordinarily attractive, he thought, as, walking across Trafalgar Square in the direction of the Haymarket, came a young woman who, as she passed Gordon's statue, seemed, Peter Walsh thought (susceptible as he was), to shed veil after veil, until she became the very woman he had always had in mind; young, but stately; merry, but discreet; black, but enchanting.[19]

With its alternation of clichéd attributes of a certain version of ideal femininity, the 'shedding of veil after veil' to reveal not so much uniqueness as indistinctness, or rather uniqueness *as* indistinctness, a fantasy 'everywoman', the passage is already bordering on parodic literary stereotype. Woolf does not let go:

> Straightening himself and stealthily fingering his pocket-knife he started after her to follow this woman, this excitement, which seemed even with its back turned to shed on him a light which connected them, which singled him out, as if the random uproar of the traffic had whispered through hallowed hands his name, not Peter, but his private name which he called himself in his own thought. 'You,' she said, only 'you,' saying it with her white gloves and her shoulders. Then the thin long cloak which the wind stirred as she walked past Dent's shop in Cockspur Street blew out with an enveloping kindness, a mournful tenderness, as of arms that would open and take the tired –
>
> (MD, 48)

The paragraph, which ends with just this uncertain and hasty dash, continues the satire, most blatantly with the fingered pocket-knife, but then with the neutralisation of 'this woman, this excitement . . . its back', and with the revelation of the 'most private' of names as the generally applicable 'you'. As in the Baudelaire poem, this woman becomes both an enfolding mother (her 'enveloping kindness', but with a hint of smothering) and a mourner.

In the next paragraph Peter wonders whether she is 'respectable'; then he imagines a meeting: ' "Come and have an ice," he would say, and she would answer perfectly simply, "Oh yes" ' (MD, 49). This happy conclusion is followed by Peter's and her metamorphosis into hero and heroine of a romantic story. Their respective sexual qualities are drawn out, by distinction or assimilation, from the window displays in the shops they pass:

> He was an adventurer, reckless, he thought, swift, daring, indeed (landed as he was last night from India) a romantic buccaneer, careless of all these damned proprieties, yellow dressing-gowns, pipes, fishing-rods, in the shop windows; and respectability and evening parties and spruce old men wearing white slips beneath their waistcoats. He was a buccaneer. On and on she went, across Piccadilly, and up Regent Street, ahead of him, her cloak, her gloves, her

shoulders combining with the fringes and the laces and the feather boas in the windows to make the spirit of finery and whimsy which dwindled out of the shops on to the pavement.

(*MD*, 49)

The displays in the luxury shops are sharply differentiated by sex. But whereas Peter's buccaneering identity is defined by its difference from the accoutrements of masculinity on display, the desirability of his quarry is seen precisely as an extension of the fetishistically feminine bits and pieces visible as they pass. Peter's proud display of himself as distinct from other men and their 'damned proprieties' is parodied in his pursuit of a femininity as predictable as the dull masculinity he is consciously refusing.

The outcome of Peter's pursuit of his *passante* is as embarrassing as that of Proust coming upon Mme Verdurin, but for a different reason:

> Laughing and delightful, she had crossed Oxford Street and Great Portland Street and turned down one of the little streets, and now, and now, the great moment was approaching, for now she slackened, opened her bag, and with one look in his direction, but not at him, one look that bade farewell, summed up the whole situation and dismissed it triumphantly, for ever, had fitted her key, opened the door, and gone!
>
> (*MD*, 49)

The passage works as the parody of the amorous clinch or climax that might have been expected: the three times culminating 'now' of 'and now, and now, the great moment was approaching, for now she slackened', as well as that of the *passante* encounter itself, with the girl's 'one look', twice named, signifying something else entirely from what the convention requires, what Peter desires. The *passante* narrative, in other words, still stands, as the dominant street story, but knowingly fictionalised: 'for it was half made up, as he knew very well; invented, this escapade with the girl; made up, as one makes up the better part of life' (*MD*, 50). Here, the look, not even at him, is nonetheless for him, indicating her understanding of the 'situation' she sums up. The inclusion of the *passante*'s angle of view has produced a parody of the genre whose conventions are clearly understood by both parties, transforming it into a gentle power game where she comes out with the victory, 'triumphantly', her bag containing a key more decisive and more serviceable than the pocket-knife, and which rapidly brings things to a close.

Peter's imaginary girl with her own latch-key and her playful rejection of standard femininity is a model New Woman; further on in *Mrs Dalloway*, Woolf offers us another version in 18-year-old Elizabeth Dalloway, whose foray on top of a bus brings her into close affinity with the daring masculinity adopted by Peter Walsh. For Elizabeth takes on the qualities of a buccaneering bus, 'the impetous creature – a pirate' (*MD*, 120), and does so by an overt distinction from the literary femininity in whose terms she is starting to be perceived: 'it was beginning. . . . People were beginning to compare her to poplar trees, early dawn, hyacinths, fawns, running water, and garden lilies' (*MD*, 119 – 20). Elizabeth's adventure on a bus is an adolescent equivalent of the dismissal of the *passante* scene accomplished by Peter Walsh's girl, in which she becomes a sort of tomboy female pirate.

These vignettes might lead us to imagine that the street-walking scene is being surreptitiously shifted, moving the *passante* out of focus to make way for something like a feminine *flânerie*. Perhaps this explains the very first words of the novel's heroine: ' "I love walking in London," said Mrs Dalloway. "Really, it's better than walking in the country" ' (*MD*, 7). What else, after all, would Clarissa's surname have led us to expect than the woman who likes to dally along the way, the *flâneuse* herself?

A ROAD OF ONE'S OWN

It might seem outlandish to think of *A Room of One's Own*, which is all about the importance of an inside, personal space for the woman writer, as having any connection with the links between women, walking and writing in Woolf's work. Yet the book is structured throughout by an imaginary ramble (through 'Oxbridge', London and the British Museum, and through many byways of bookish history), leading up to the point at which the narrator represents herself sitting down to start writing what she has just recounted. The literal and the recorded walk thus overlay one another so as to play upon the difficulty of differentiating them. As with *A la recherche du temps perdu*, the circular structure is such that the end sends you straight back to the beginning; but Proust's novel is not set out, as is *A Room of One's Own*, as a *flânerie*. For Woolf, it is as though casual walking were the only possible way of dealing with such an intractable subject for a lecture as 'women and fiction'.

A Room of One's Own has many direct evocations of this fictional stroll. 'I had come at last, in the course of this rambling, to the shelves which hold books by the living' (*ROO*, 79); 'And with Mrs Behn, we turn a very important corner in the road' (*ROO*, 64); 'I spare you the twists and turns of my cogitations, for no conclusion was found on the road to Headingley' (*ROO*, 17). The figure of rambling serves to suggest the argument which turns into the narrative of its own lack of an ending:

> I have shirked the duty of coming to a conclusion upon these questions – women and fiction remain, so far as I am concerned, unsolved problems. But in order to make some amends I am going to do what I can to show you how I arrived at this opinion about the room and the money.
>
> (*ROO*, 6)

'How I arrived', in the context of the general language of strolling and rambling, exposes one of a whole clutch of metaphors which writers and readers normally pass by without a second glance. Introduction, digression, excursus, passage: it is as though the very grounds of rhetoric were made for walking on, measured out in properly poetical metres and feet.

But there are also stopping points in Woolf's text where the city walk provides a more elaborated analogy for the writer's stamping ground:

> There came to my mind's eye one of those long streets somewhere south of the river whose infinite rows are innumerably populated. With the eye of the imagination I saw a very ancient lady crossing the street on the arm of a middle-aged woman, her daughter, perhaps, both so respectably booted and furred that their dressing in the afternoon must be a ritual . . .
>
> (*ROO*, 88)

What starts here as a typical ('one of those') and imaginary ('in my mind's eye') street soon becomes specific and actual, with the narrator acting as though it were not in her own power to determine the description or meaning of the characters 'I saw'. The scene then becomes a question of precise specification:

> The elder is close on eighty. . . . And if one asked her, longing to pin down the moment with date and season, But what were you doing on the fifth of April 1868, or the second of November 1875, she would look vague and say that she could remember nothing. For all the dinners are cooked; the plates and cups washed; the children sent to school and gone out into the world. Nothing remains of it all. All has vanished. No biography or history has a word to say about it. And the novels, without meaning to, inevitably lie.
>
> (ROO, 89)

The disingenuousness of this is blatant: the lady is a fictional invention to begin with – a projection, perhaps of the 'over-excited imagination' of the woman writer. But that is only to say that the usual fiction that the subject is not a fiction – as though the narrator had simply said 'I saw an old lady of eighty' – has here been shown up. Though the final sentences seem to deplore the absence of solid written evidence for the woman's everyday life, or else its distortion in the novels which 'inevitably lie', the self-consciously fictional framing of the argument undermines the possibility of differentiating the facts from the errors. This gives a quite distinct cast to the proposal for future writing projects:

> All these infinitely obscure lives remain to be recorded, I said . . . and went on in thought through the streets of London feeling in imagination the pressure of dumbness, the accumulation of unrecorded life, whether from the women at the street corners with their arms akimbo, and the rings embedded in their fat swollen fingers, talking with a gesticulation like the swing of Shakespeare's words; or from the violet-sellers and match-sellers and old crones stationed under doorways; or from drifting girls whose faces, like waves in sun and cloud, signal the coming of men and women and the flickering lights of shop windows.
>
> (ROO, 89)

Some very unexpected moves are going on here. It is a self-conscious poeticisation of the never before recorded lives which first suggests itself, through the Shakespearean gestures or the girls with faces 'like waves in sun and cloud', as though Woolf were pointing out the risks of assuming that words could act as a pristine or undistorted medium for the new records demanded of them. And then, the unrecordedness of the lives is in the eyes or the 'feeling' of the beholder, who, as in the case of the old lady and her daughter, is only a beholder 'in imagination'. She hereby records what she declares at once unrecorded (a presumed fact) and fictional (her own invention). What looks to the eye of the reader like a predictable call for indiscriminate documentary detail is actually a passage which creates all sorts of complications about the claims of documentary writing and the claims or place of the documentary observer.

So when, elsewhere in *A Room of One's Own*, the narrator speaks of 'the fascination of the London street' (*ROO*, 94), or when she urges her audience of Newnham College students to 'loiter at street corners' as one of the means 'to write all kinds of books' (*ROO*, 107), she is advocating a form of female street-walking or street-writing which is clearly going to deviate from any expected routes. It is not so straightforward a matter to urge that women make up for lost time, even though that is also part of the plea; and it is not evident that one woman can simply call for or advocate the representation of other women as though that were a neutral question of inclusion and access, as though the writer objectively picked out and covered a topic or subject that was simply there, awaiting but not to be modified by her attention.

'STREET HAUNTING'

In a diary entry from May 1928, Woolf wrote: 'London itself perpetually attracts, stimulates, gives me a play and a story and a poem, without any trouble, save that of moving my legs through the streets'.[20] The essay entitled 'Street Haunting: A London Adventure' (1927) is probably her most graphic development of this statement. The piece dramatises the evening walk through the streets of London of a narrator constantly fabricating or recording the stories around her; walking the streets be-comes, in effect, the background or ground for story-making (at once, and indistinguishably, its necessary preliminary or pre-amble and its milieu, the place of the story). At the outset – setting off – the narrator declares, disingenuously, that her sortie involves a purely spurious object, an 'excuse for walking half across London between tea and dinner' to justify the pleasure.[21] That object is nothing else than the purchase of a pencil, of the means of writing. At the end of the essay the appointed purchase is duly made, after the narrator has entered a stationer's for the purpose (the purpose of fulfilling the fake purpose). There are two other shops she goes into during the course of her wanderings. Given the connection made in the diary between writing and walking, and given that the pencil is already taken care of, it seems wholly fitting that one of these should be a boot shop. But we are getting ahead of ourselves and must first retrace our steps to the start of the essay/adventure.

Leaving the house is accompanied, for the narrator, by a loss of personal identity:

> We are no longer quite ourselves. As we step out of the house on a fine evening between four and six, we shed the self our friends know us by and become part of that vast republican army of anonymous trampers, whose society is so agreeable after the solitude of one's own room.
>
> (CE, 4: 155)

The move outside involves the removal of individuality for anonymity, and the shift from stability – one fixed place – to mobility, a peaceable 'army' on the move. Already there are some odd shifts here: 'ourselves' is equivocally identified with the projection or externalisation of 'the self our friends know us by'. The friends are associated with the house that is being temporarily left; but then it turns out that pleasant companionship ('agreeable' 'society') is actually to be found out of doors and among the 'anonymous'. On the very threshold of her walk, the narrator has already effected some striking displacements which should serve as hints of what is to come.

This shedding of self will quickly be given another simile, another walking attribute:

> The shell-like covering which our souls have excreted to house themselves, to make for themselves a shape distinct

from others, is broken, and there is left of all these wrinkles and roughnesses a central oyster of perceptiveness, an enormous eye. How beautiful a street is in winter!

(CE, 4: 156)

A corollary, then, of the move from self to anonymity is the change from 'I' to eye, from pronoun to organ, the recording eye of 'a central oyster of perceptiveness'.[22] A little further on, we discover more of its attributes. First, this is an eye which looks to surfaces, not to an in-depth examination:

> But, after all, we are only gliding smoothly on the surface. The eye is not a miner, not a diver, not a seeker after buried treasure. It floats us smoothly down a stream; resting, pausing, the brain perhaps sleeps as it looks. . . .
> But here we must stop peremptorily. We are in danger of digging deeper than the eye approves; we are impeding our passage down the smooth stream by catching at some branch or root. . . . Let us dally a little longer, be content still with surfaces only.

(CE, 4. 156—7)

The surface looking advocated here does not imply that there is no depth, but that its evasion is part of what defines the pleasures of all-eye looking. Dallying is superficial, 'surfaces only'. To dig deeper, far from being an obligation, is a danger.

And this leads on to one final characteristic: the spontaneous aestheticism of this roving eye:

> For the eye has this strange property: it rests only on beauty; like a butterfly it seeks colour and basks in warmth. On a winter's night like this, when nature has been at pains to polish and preen herself, it brings back the prettiest trophies, breaks off little lumps of emerald and coral as if the whole earth were made of precious stone. The thing it cannot do (one is speaking of the average unprofessional eye) is to compose these trophies in such a way as to bring out the more obscure angles and relationships. Hence after a prolonged diet of this simple sugary fare, of beauty pure and uncomposed, we become conscious of satiety. We halt at the door of the boot shop.

(CE, 4: 157)

Here the eye has become a mouth, a consumer of sweet things, 'sugary fare'. There is a frivolity, an avowed superficiality, shared in common by the spectator (the eye 'like a butterfly') and the surface from which it takes its selection ('the prettiest trophies'). The flirtatiousness of nature, 'at pains to polish and preen herself' seems to rub off her synaesthetic sensuality onto the 'butterfly' eye which seeks not only colour but warmth and touch (it 'breaks off little lumps').

The superficial sauntering of this eye finds its most perfect expression or egression in window-shopping. The first example has already suggested this:

> Let us dally a little longer, be content still with surfaces only – the glossy brilliance of the motor omnibuses; the carnal splendour of the butchers' shops with their yellow flanks and purple steaks; the blue and red bunches of flowers burning so bravely through the plate glass of the florists' windows.
>
> (CE, 4: 157)

Colour, the surface view, takes precedence over distinctions of substance, say between meat and flowers. The transparency of the plate-glass windows seems, like the glossy omnibuses, to go along with a deliberate indulgence in purely visual pleasures at the expense of all else.

At the expense, in fact, of expense: this process is extended even further when looking in shop windows is represented as a pleasurable end in itself, unconnected with a potential purchase:

> Passing, glimpsing, everything seems accidentally but miraculously sprinkled with beauty, as if the tide of trade which deposits its burden so punctually and prosaically upon the shores of Oxford Street had this night cast up nothing but treasure. With no thought of buying, the eye is sportive and generous; it creates, it adorns; it enhances. Standing out in the street, one may build up all the chambers of an imaginary house and furnish them at one's will with sofa, table, carpet.
>
> (CE, 4: 160)

The 'treasure' here is not excavated, the depth beneath a surface, but 'cast up' spontaneously. 'Passing, glimpsing', the *passante* has become the mobile spectator herself, not the one who is glimpsed, her active looking making an implicit contrast with what now appears to have been the passivity of the woman seen by the masculine *flâneur*.

But this is not the only possible reading of 'Street Haunting'. To read it like this involves just the same kind of selectivity as the eye is supposed to perform, with its 'butterfly' flitting to and fro, alighting only on what pleases it, or even imagining what suits it: 'it creates'. Pursuing a different trail, we would see quite other things along the way of Woolf's essay. Its title, after all, might suggest that there is more going on than a simple, naive delight. 'Haunting' is almost a homonym of one of the possible English words for translating *flâner*: 'sauntering'. In a diary entry from a few years before, Woolf had written: 'I like this London life in early summer – the street sauntering & square haunting' (D, 3: 11; 20.4.1925), as if bringing the two terms into complete synonymity, neighbours of sense as well as sound. But 'haunting', in its ordinary usage, is anything but a casual, strolling word. The essay that so vehemently advocates looking only at surfaces is also, by that very exaggeration, indicating that such an attitude may be hiding something else too.

Reading with less accommodating eyes, we spot other details. At first, indifferently, as we have seen, the narrator left her house and her 'self' to 'become part of that vast republican army of anonymous trampers, whose society is so agreeable after the solitude of one's own room' (CE, 4: 155). A few pages on, her companions have been metamorphosed into 'this maimed company of the halt and the blind' (CE, 4: 159). The section immediately prior to the passage on window-shopping reads as follows:

> They do not grudge us, we are musing, our prosperity; when, suddenly, turning the corner, we come upon a bearded Jew, wild, hunger-bitten, glaring out of his misery; or pass the humped body of an old woman flung abandoned on the step of a public building with a cloak over her like a hasty covering thrown over a dead horse or a donkey. At such sights the nerves of the spine seem to stand erect; a sudden flare is brandished in our eyes; a question is asked which is never answered.

At the beginning it looks as though the self-consciously

reassuring suggestion that 'they' are content with their inferiority to the observer is to be turned into a restatement of a clear-cut difference, but of another kind, as 'they' become desperate, even dead, animals. But the grotesque is twisted in an unexpected direction here. The wildness of the 'sights' is reciprocated in the bestialisation of the genteel spectator too, reduced or transformed to a body of instinctual responses: 'the nerves of the spine seem to stand erect'. The passage continues:

> Often enough these derelicts choose to lie not a stone's-throw from theatres, within hearing of barrel organs, almost, as night draws on, within touch of the sequined cloaks and bright legs of diners and dancers. They lie close to those shop-windows where commerce offers to a world of old women laid on doorsteps, of blind men, of hobbling dwarfs, sofas which are supported by the gilt necks of proud swans; tables inlaid with baskets of many-coloured fruit; sideboards paved with green marble the better to support the weight of boars' heads; and carpets so softened with age that their carnations have almost vanished in a pale-green sea.
>
> (CE, 4: 159–60)

Preceded by this extreme juxtaposition, the 'Passing, glimpsing' paragraph becomes open to, if it does not demand, other readings. It is going to haunt the harmless pleasures of window-shopping. One way of looking at the relationship, clearly, would be as that of an implicit reprimand to the luxury-loving spectator. But here again, as in the earlier section, there is not a contrast but a rapprochement, even an identification, and in more than one way. The 'derelicts' freely 'choose' their position, and it is to them that 'commerce offers' its exhibition. They are not beggars but ideal consumers. And the more prosperous narrator, by her own account, is not looking to buy, but only to look, using what is on view in the windows as a basis for pure fantasy: she is only going to buy a practical pencil. The curious individuals who 'choose to lie' near the theatres and shops are 'sights' for strolling eyes, but they are also themselves connoisseurs of the pleasures of spectacle for its own sake. And though the narrator does not see herself as seen by them, the path of her own description has had the effect of abolishing the difference it initially sets up.

From this perspective, we can turn to two particularly odd trios encountered *en route*. Inside the boot shop, the casual walker is cut down to size:

> We halt at the door of the boot shop and make some little excuse, which has nothing to do with the real reason, for folding up the bright paraphernalia of the streets and withdrawing to some duskier chamber of the being where we may ask, as we raise our left foot obediently upon the stand: 'What, then, is it like to be a dwarf?'
>
> (CE, 4: 157)

Here the difference of indoors and outdoors makes the streets equivalent to the butterfly's wings, their display an extension of the walker who is at liberty to fold them up for her withdrawal inside. The interior of the shop is represented as a place of infantilisation, of fitting conformity 'as we raise our left foot obediently', in which the footloose *flâneuse* is brought abruptly to a standstill. In this light, the question 'What is it like to be a dwarf?' acquires enough of a rationale for its literal explanation, in the next sentence, to come as a surprise:

> She came in escorted by two women who, being of normal size, looked like benevolent giants beside her. Smiling at the shop-girls, they seemed to be disclaiming any lot in her deformity and assuring her of their protection. She wore the peevish yet apologetic expression usual on the faces of the deformed. She needed their kindness, yet resented it.
>
> (CE, 4: 157–8)

So far, the female dwarf is still a curiosity, and also a type, wearing the 'expression usual on the faces of the deformed'. But then her pride in her feet alters the focus to hers as she stands unique among an undifferentiated audience of 'us':

> Look at that! Look at that! she seemed to demand of us all, as she thrust her foot out, for behold it was the shapely, perfectly proportioned foot of a well-grown woman. It was arched; it was aristocratic. . . . Her manner became full of self-confidence. She sent for shoe after shoe. . . . She got up and pirouetted before a glass which reflected the foot only in yellow shoes, in fawn shoes, in shoes of lizard-skin. . . . She was thinking that, after all, feet are the most important part

of the whole person; women, she said to herself, have been loved for their feet alone.

(CE, 4: 158)

This is a wonderful turning upon ordinary viewpoints, as the female dwarf, already diminished in the common perception, is shown to aggrandise herself by an identification with an even slighter part, her feet alone, classic choice of male fetishism; and by means of what might be assumed to be her weakest point, the figure of the narcissistic woman, parading in front of the glass for her own admiration. Instead of a surface/depth structure, in which the appearance of abnormality or deficiency is represented as none the less concealing an inner virtue or beauty (the pure heart or soul within), the surface look which it might have been thought tactful to disregard is highlighted as the very image of perfection. Unerringly, the dwarf puts her best foot forward, thereby transforming the narrator's own view: 'she had changed the mood; she had called into being an atmosphere which, as we followed her out into the street, seemed actually to create the humped, the twisted, the deformed' (CE, 4: 158).

Woolf's transformation of the small woman into the epitome of a proud, surefooted femininity perversely plays on other representations of the grotesque and of the feminine, the impact of the passage deriving from the way in which the negative connotations of each are dramatically inverted. The impression that Woolf is playing with distortions of sexual perspective is reinforced by the sighting, immediately on leaving the boot shop, of a second, equally bizarre, single-sex trio: 'Two bearded men, brothers, apparently, stone-blind, supporting themselves by resting a head on the small boy between them, marched down the street' (CE. 4: 158). There is something deliberately staged in the symmetrical contrasts here: two groups, one female, one male, formed to protect a disability, the one in the middle being the sufferer in the first case (the dwarf), and the support (the little boy) in the second. In the second group, the two on the outside are the blind; in the first group the 'outsider', the dwarf, is on the inside. But this focused formal perfection is not left as an aesthetic spectacle. It moves out to take over the onlookers as well:

As they passed, holding straight on, the little convoy seemed to cleave asunder the passers-by, with the momentum of its silence, its directness, its disaster. Indeed, the dwarf had started a hobbling grotesque dance to which everybody in the street had now conformed; the stout lady tightly swathed in shiny seal-skin; the feeble-minded boy sucking the silver knob of his stick; the old man squatted on the doorstep as if, suddenly overcome by the absurdity of the human spectacle, he had sat down to look at it – all joined in the hobble and tap of the dwarf's dance.

(CE, 4: 159)

This is a scene quite similar to the one in *Between the Acts* in which the audience of the village play are forced, by means of mirrors turned in their direction, to see themselves as part of the spectacle, not its comfortably external observers. The street 'scene' here becomes precisely the place where the simple stereotypical distinctions associated with anonymous encounters and visual judgements are broken down. Everyone is grotesque, just as all the seeming poor can turn out from one point of view to be equivalent to affluent consumers.

My suggestion here is not that Woolf is making a moral point about the harmony of all mankind, whether wealthy or impoverished, disabled or healthy, or, on the other hand, that she is wilfully disregarding the effects of social and physical differences; nor is she using a form of ironic assimilation to emphasise these differences all the more. All these possibilities are present in the way that the scenes are narrated, but they are exposed as limited, much as the artificially distinguished sexual groupings point by exaggeration to the inadequacies of the habitual binary division. Like Aristophanes' three sexes, Woolf's curious trios and types show up the normal orders in an unfamiliar light.

But there is a third shop entered along the narrator's way: a second-hand bookshop. Placed between the two other shop scenes, this episode has the function, by position as well as by subject matter, of a *mise en abîme* of this ambulatory inventiveness: 'Second-hand books are wild books, homeless books; they have come together in vast flocks of variegated feather, and have a charm which the domesticated volumes of the library lack' (CE, 4: 161). Most of the volumes randomly perused turn out to be accounts of foreign travel, 'so restless the English are'

(CE, 4: 162), and their printed narratives, of which random fragments are gleaned here and there in a few minutes' browsing, are identified with the casual encounters of the walk in London:

> The number of books in the world is infinite, and one is forced to glimpse and nod and move on after a moment of talk, a flash of understanding, as, in the street outside, one catches a word in passing and from a chance phrase fabricates a lifetime.
>
> (CE, 4: 163)

The street here is one of words, just as the book is a passing street acquaintance, briefly sighted, from which we 'move on'. Woolf's essay is rounded off with the expected purchase of a pencil, it being declared from the outset that this object is a mere excuse for the walk in which her narrator has meanwhile been indulging. But of course the point of the pencil is a sharper one than this allows. The shoes and the pencil suggest the connection between walking and writing, between strolling and story-making, which the other two shops, with their footwear and literary wares, reinforce: these boots are made for writing.

The essay ends with a celebration of walking as fantasy, as creative mobility:

> Walking home through the desolation one could tell oneself the story of the dwarf, of the blind men, of the party in the Mayfair mansion, of the quarrel in the stationer's shop. Into each of these lives one could penetrate a little way, far enough to give oneself the illusion that one is not tethered to a single mind, but can put on briefly for a few minutes the bodies and minds of others. . . . And what greater delight and wonder can there be than to leave the straight lines of personality and deviate into those footpaths that lead beneath brambles and thick tree trunks into the heart of the forest where live those wild beasts, our fellow men?
>
> (CE, 4: 165)

This is not, once again, so easy an affirmation as it looks: 'those wild beasts, our fellow men' include the walker who knows she is only giving herself 'the illusion' of not being 'tethered to a single spot': her imaginative freedom is qualified as that of an animal in reality tied to its place, its imaginary other identifications starting from there. But the valorisation of deviation over the straight line itself makes way for a transformation here of conventional comparison. Covertly displacing the usual opposition between the artificial city and primitive country, it is the urban landscape which becomes a natural wilderness.

Before finishing with Woolf's walking text, let us just note in passing a moment in the 'Street Haunting' essay where the narrator seems to put the clamp on the open and fluid identification which she is elsewhere suggesting. The passage takes a very standard, direct-line route to the suburbs south of London:

> The main stream of walkers at this hour sweeps too fast to let us ask such questions. They are wrapt, in this short passage from work to home, in some narcotic dream, now that they are free from the desk and have the fresh air on their cheeks. They put on those bright clothes which they must hang up and lock the key upon all the rest of the day, and are great cricketers, famous actresses, soldiers who have saved their country at the hour of need. Dreaming, gesticulating, often muttering a few words aloud, they sweep over the Strand and across Waterloo Bridge whence they will be slung in long rattling trains, to some prim little villa in Barnes or Surbiton where the sight of the clock in the hall and the smell of the supper in the basement puncture the dream.
>
> (CE, 4: 163)

Woolf's representation of the commuter crowd takes a conventional distance, through its predictable representation of bourgeois conventionality. It first promises, as with the other encounters of the evening walk, to complicate the stereotype, making the rush-hour into a time of escape, of dreaming. But then the homogeneous crowd is swiftly dismissed into the standardised horrors of 'some prim little villa', where the narrator seems positively to turn up her nose at 'the smell of the supper in the basement'. If the habitual representations of the Victorian 'nether world' of the back streets of London can be questioned successfully and rendered differently, Woolf's narrator seems to stop short when it comes to imagining suburbia as other than a nightmare when viewed from what now becomes the safe preserve of the sophisticated inner-city gaze.

Near the beginning, I drew a distinction between two approaches or walks toward a conception of women's writing: as a question of progress, forward along a given line, or a question of a transgressiveness implicit in the position outside that of masculine normality. In tracing a path that goes from Baudelaire to Proust to Woolf, I have been running or walking both these questions together. On the one hand, it will have seemed that all roads lead to Woolf, to the culmination of a certain tradition of writing about walking and women in the eventual arrival of the woman writer herself in the first part of the twentieth century. On the other hand, in suggesting that Woolf's writing upsets the persepectives of writing itself, and of the representation of the sexes, I have been implying that this questioning reaches no settled identity, but that there might be reasons for calling it feminine, in relation to what it exposes as a masculine norm.

I cannot conclude by smoothly bringing about a meeting between these two alternatives; and it may be their very tension which allows for some movement. At the same time, they are inadequate as alternatives, derived from conceptions of historical change and the difference of the sexes which decide the possible questions in advance, before the chance encounters of the walk. If, as I have been suggesting, there is no simple way forward for the *passante* as woman writer, nor is there an impasse, a block, a simple impediment. There may also be returns and double, even triple times and spaces of walking and writing. The ghosts that come back to trouble the familiar pictures of the modern street are a threat, but also, perhaps, and for the same reason, a way of going somewhere else.

NOTES

Shorter versions of this chapter appear in *Tropismes*, 5, special issue on *L'Errance* (1991), 207–32, and in Isobel Armstrong (ed.), *New Feminist Discourses* (London: Routledge, 1992).
1 See Plato, *The Symposium*, trans. Walter Hamilton (Harmondsworth: Penguin, 1951), pp. 58–65.
2 Freud, *Three Essays on the Theory of Sexuality* (1905) Pelican Freud Library, vol. 7 (Harmondsworth: Penguin, 1977), p.46.
3 Virginia Woolf, *A Room of One's Own* (1928; rpt. Harmondsworth: Penguin, 1967), p.27. Further references will be included within the

text, abbreviating the title to 'ROO'.

4 For an analysis of the absence in terms of women's exclusion from the newly formed 'public sphere' of modernity, see Janet Wolff, 'The invisible *flâneuse*', *Theory, Culture and Society*, vol. 2, no. 3 (1985), 37–46.

5 'The foreign loiterer consumes the innumerable curiosities of the place [the Jardin des Plantes] quite at his ease. He carefully counts up all the pebbles in the mineralogical gallery, all the more or less exotic grasses in the natural history collection, he calculates how many shirt-buttons you could make with the elephant's tusks. . . .The foreign loiterer said to himself when he was getting up in the morning, "Today I will see eleven monuments!" Provided that when he does his sums in the evening he does indeed manage to tot up his eleven monuments, he thinks that he hasn't wasted his day and he goes to sleep with a conscience as well satisfied as that of Titus himself. The foreign loiterer hardly arrives in front of his monument before he hardly takes the time to raise his eyes to the columns or other accessories, it being expected that out of the five minutes granted to the said monument, he allots four of them to the reading of the description given of it in the *Traveller's Guide*.' Louis Huart, *Le Flâneur* (Paris: Aubert, 1850, 'Bibliothèque pour rire' collection, with '70 vignettes de MM. Alophe, Daumier, et Maurisset'), chapter VI. Further references will be given within the text.

6 'Where one proves that the *flâneur* is an essentially virtuous mortal'.

7 'An uninterrupted series of green shutters'.

8 '*Flâneries* taken in the company of a woman are even more to be avoided.
   "What! Even with a pretty woman, you're telling me?"
   "Yes, sir; and especially with a pretty woman!"
   For women do not understand *flâneries* and stoppings-off, except in front of the hats in the fashion shops and the seamstresses' bonnets – when it isn't in front of the cashmere things and other trifles, the mere sight of which sends a shiver through any husband, or any other young Frenchman carrying out a roughly comparable job. When one takes one's wife or mistress to the Tuileries or to a show, the most economical plan is to take a cab. The unfortunate fellow who wants to make this saving of thirty-six sous runs the risk of paying instead for a thirty-two franc hat – or else of seeming like a miser, or a somewhat ungallant male being.'

9 'Talk to me about the Tuileries and the Champs-Elysées! There you have some places for walks where at least one finds everything that makes for *flâneurs*' delights: we mean women, trees, children, crowds, and Punch and Judy!'

10 'You're wanting to follow a simple working girl, while your co-*flâneur* would have you run over or, worse than that, covered in mud by the carriage of a great lady he had wanted to admire too close up.'

11 'We forgive the fondness for the milliner, all tastes are natural, but we think this fondness should not be pushed to the point of fanaticism. So the *flâneur* is perfectly justified in following with his eye the young milliner who, using the name of Trottin, will bring

charming little hats and adorable little hoods to your home; but you always have to exercise reserve and discretion.'

12 'Do not imitate those crude characters who follow women in a brazen manner; conduct of this kind is punishable by all truly Frrrrench boots. Instead of walking all over the heels of virtue, set yourself up as the defender, the protector, of this same frightened virtue, which comes to take shelter near you like a poor panting dove, to escape the pursuits of those ignoble men who insult all women.'

13 He is no *flâneur* or does not know how to be – who walks fast; who yawns in the street; who passes in front of a pretty woman without looking at her, in front of a shop display or an acrobat without stopping. The real *flâneur* has the right to be ignorant of Greek, Latin, mathematics and the other scientific superfluities; but he must be familiar with all the streets, all the shops of Paris, know precisely who is the prettiest hat-seller, hat-maker, delicatessen assistant, waitress, etc., etc.'

14 Baudelaire, *Les Fleurs du Mal* (1861); rpt. in *Oeuvres Complètes* (Paris: Seuil, 1968), p. 101.

> The deafening street around me was shouting.
> Tall, slim, in heavy mourning, majestic grief,
> A woman passed, with a proud hand
> Lifting, balancing the garland and the hem;
>
> Agile and noble, with her statuesque leg.
> Me, I was drinking, clenched like a madman,
> In her eye, livid sky where the hurricane germinates,
> The gentleness that fascinates and the pleasure that kills.
>
> One flash . . . then night! Fugitive beauty
> Whose look made me suddenly reborn,
> Will I see you no more but in eternity?
>
> Elsewhere, very far from here! too late! *never* perhaps!
> For I know not where you are fleeing, you know not where I am
>   going,
> O you whom I would have loved, o you who knew it!

15 I borrow this phrase from Walter Benjamin, who speaks in relation to this poem of 'eine Liebe nicht sowohl auf den ersten als auf den letzten Blick', a 'love not at first sight, but at last sight', in 'On some motifs in Baudelaire', *Illuminations*, trans. Harry Zohn (New York: Schocken, 1969), p. 169.

16 Proust, *À l'ombre des jeunes filles en fleur* II (Paris: Garnier Flammarion, 1987), p. 87.

> The charms of the *passante* are generally directly related to the rapidity of the passing. It only takes night to be falling and the vehicle to be going fast, in the country, in a city, and there is not one female torso, mutilated like an ancient marble by the speed that carries us forward and the dusk which darkens it, which does

not aim at our heart, at every corner on the way, in the depths of every shop, the arrows of Beauty, of Beauty of which it might sometimes be tempting to wonder whether in this world it is anything else but the complementary part added to a fragmentary and fugitive *passante* by our imagination overexcited by regret.

17 Proust uses the word himself in another *passante* passage, referring to 'une projection . . . un mirage du désir', *À l'ombre*, II, p. 182.
18 *A l'ombre*, II, pp. 87–8.

Never in my life have I encountered such desirable girls as the days when I was with some serious person whom, in spite of the thousands of pretexts I made up, I could not leave: some years after the one when I went for the first time to Balbec, in a vehicle doing an errand with a friend of my father's in Paris and having caught sight of a woman walking quickly in the night, I thought it was unreasonable to lose for reasons of propriety my share of happiness in what is no doubt the only life there is, and leaping down without a word of apology, I set off in search of the unknown woman, lost her at the crossroads of two streets, found her again in a third one, and found myself, finally, completely out of breath, under a lamp-post, opposite old Madame Verdurin whom I was avoiding everywhere and who, surprised and happy, exclaimed: 'Oh! how kind to have run up to say hello to me!'

19 Woolf, *Mrs Dalloway* (1922; rpt. London: Granada, 1976), p.48. Further references will be included in the text as '*MD*'.
20 *The Diary of Virginia Woolf*, vol. 3, 1925–30, ed. Anne Olivier Bell (1980; rpt. Harmondsworth: Penguin, 1982), p. 186; entry for 31.5.1928.
21 Woolf, *Collected Essays*, ed. Leonard Woolf, vol. IV (London: Chatto & Windus, 1967), p. 155. Further references will be included in the text, as '*CE*: 4'. This essay will be reprinted in Woolf's *The Crowded Dance of Modern Life: Selected Essays, vol. 2*, ed. Rachel Bowlby (Harmondsworth: Penguin, 1993).
22 This 'central oyster of perceptiveness' seems an extraordinarily enigmatic expression. Apart from the closeness of 'oy-eye-I', the oyster itself seems to include suggestions of sensory responsiveness (of the animal itself) and voluptuousness (the pleasure of the consumer). Webster's dictionary defines the oyster as 'a marine bivalve mollusk (family Ostreidae) having a rough irregular shell closed by a single adductor muscle, the foot small or wanting, and no siphon, living free on the bottom or adhering to stones or other objects in shallow water along the seacoasts or in brackish water in the mouths of rivers, and feeding on minute plants or animals carried to them by the current'. The specification of 'the foot small or wanting' is not irrelevant to the theme of feminine strolling, and in particular to one of the episodes of Woolf's essay discussed below; that Woolf's street should be in a sense submarine accords with an insistent imagery that surfaces throughout her writing.

Chapter 2

The impasse
Jean Rhys's Good Morning, Midnight

After the movements that seemed to be occurring in Virginia Woolf's writing, Jean Rhys appears, during the same period between the wars, to be situating her women in social and psychical places that are oppressively constant and claustrophobic. In a phrase that occurs in *Good Morning, Midnight* at the confluence of personal nightmare and public urban directive, there is simply no 'way out' from something whose difficulty cannot even begin to be named. Rhys's novels seem to give the lie, to mock as mere drawing-room fantasy, the bright hopes of new women's stories, or even the bright hopes of stories of progress at all. Her heroines drift around the cities of Europe in states of melancholy from which they seem unable to escape. They revolve in a mental universe where nothing seems to change, all times are the same, and their social world, a repeated succession of failed jobs, failed love and failing feminine appearance, seems perfectly fitted to reflect or to have produced this psychic predicament.

Recent feminist writers on Rhys seem to respond to the way that her novels of this time[1] appear both to demand and to render impossible the imposition of a clear-cut interpretation. For Rhys, even more than with other writers, it does not seem easy to decide that her heroines' troubles are supposed to be caused by this or by that, by men, or madness, or the commodification of women in modern capitalism.[2] Conclusions which – to use a phrase which, as we shall see, is full of resonance in *Good Morning, Midnight* – might move things onto a different plane seem forced, to the same extent that the novels themselves seem both to seek and to deem out of reach some possible order or plan which would make sense of them as narratives in which one thing can be securely related to another in terms of time or cause. It is as though there were a continuous possibility of slumping back into some state of undifferentiation from which the attempt at a particular story – of this woman, these places, these times – has only artificially and momentarily managed to emerge. This is what I will try, haltingly, to describe, in an account which in some ways can only repeat Rhys's own sense of stories as unstories, static and slow repeats.

ON THE SAME PLANE

Good Morning, Midnight begins where it ends, ends where it begins: in the same room, outside a street which is 'what they call an impasse'.[3] At the start, it is the room that speaks, in the first words of the novel. ' "Quite like old times," the room says. "Yes? No?" ' At the end there is someone else in the room. It is not clear whether he is a third person (since the room speaks) or any person (since he is a figure who has been represented throughout in images likening him to death, a skeleton, a ghost). It is to him that the narrator of the novel addresses the last word:

> He doesn't say anything. Thank God, he doesn't say anything. I look straight into his eyes and despise another human being for the last time. For the last time. . . .
>   Then I put my arms round him and pull him down on to the bed, saying: 'Yes – yes – yes.'
>
> (190)

From the open ' "Yes? No?" ' coming from elsewhere to the decided ' "Yes – yes – yes" ' spoken by the narrator there might seem to have been a progression. The impasse has perhaps ceased to serve as a block, and the narrator has made her way somewhere else, returning to the same room differently. For here she is, after all, with a lover, speaking the lines of Molly Bloom's affirmation at the end of *Ulysses*.

But in the light of the double occurrences of 'he doesn't say anything' and 'for the last time', the triple 'yes' offers no sense of a positive iteration. This use of the present tense goes with a paratactical structure at the level of the sentences.[4] There are commas, there is one phrase and then the next, in fairly short sentences. There are no colons or semicolons to suggest specific or complex causal or other relations between clauses. Ellipses are everywhere, as though such connections might have been left out, or as though there was no way that they could ever securely be made. As with the previous sentence, Rhys will sometimes put forward a series of possible causes – 'perhaps because, or perhaps because. . .' There is no suggestion of a criterion for distinguishing between them, but their mere listing, as possible causes, brings out the absence of the usual narrative protocols.

Similarly the time for the most part is one time, the present, even in the sections recounting scenes which are past. This temporal levelling is registered most starkly in relation to the primary markers of differential time, birth and death. When Sasha's baby died, the mother was swathed in bandages to make her 'just as you were before':

> When I complain about the bandages she says: 'I promise you that when you take them off you'll be just as you were before.' And it is true. When she takes them off there is not one line, not one wrinkle, not one crease.
>
> And five weeks afterwards there I am, with not one line, not one wrinkle, not one crease.
>
> And there he is, lying with a ticket tied round his wrist because he died in a hospital. And there I am looking down at him, without one line, without one wrinkle, without one crease. . . .
>
> (60–1)

The mother is as immaculate as a newborn child, but birth means death. Her repair is no new beginning, no step beyond or in place of the baby's life. There is nothing but a switch of positions, though it is not even clear that the positions were separate in the first place, at the first time. In the same way, the conjunction which closes the book occurs between two lifeless bodies, between the one who is 'like the ghost of the landing' (14) and the one who waits for him now 'as still as if I were dead' (190).

This absence of differentiation between times or between life and death extends to or parallels the representation of spaces. The effect is a kind of platitude, a flattening, in which everything resembles everything else with the identical sameness of a cliché.[5] 'Quite like old times', making one present appear barely distinguishable from others, goes along with the relative sameness of rooms, streets, cities – and persons. For persons, it is already clear, are not easily differentiated from inanimate things. It is not so much that the speaking room is personified, as that the person is first like a room, or like any other identifiable external object (a mirror may speak, or a street).

Near the beginning, a comment is attributed to Sidonie,[6] the London friend who sent Sasha over for her two weeks in Paris, which seems to declare by negation this narrative principle of undifferentiation that extends to objects, places, times and to the phrases which mark them out in their flat resemblances:

> But one mustn't put everything on the same plane. That's her great phrase. And one mustn't put everybody on the same plane, either. Of course not. And this is my plane. . . . Quatrième à gauche, and mind you don't trip over the hole in the carpet. That's me.
> There are some black specks on the wall. I stare at them, certain they are moving. Well, I ought to be able to ignore a few bugs by this time. 'Il ne faut pas mettre tout sur le même plan. . . .'

(12)

As with 'Quite like old times' at the beginning, this remark is set off as being a cliché. It is the kind of thing people say. It can turn nasty, bug the smoothness of common sense, by the slightest touch of the ironic distance which adds to the phrase the acknowledgement that it is a cliché. This has been said before, and not by me, though perhaps by me too. It is not an individual statement or one specific to this place and this time. 'Quite like old times', opening the novel with an illusion to 'Just like old times', has the tiny change that sets off and sours a familiar phrase as a sentimental wish. The sentimental wish is mocked as already a cliché, and mourned as the absence of such a wish. 'One mustn't put everything on the same plane', reproduced in translation, putting two languages on the same plane, and presented as a repeated utterance ('That's her great phrase'), applicable to anything. And everything is thereby put on the same plane.

The possibility of putting things on a different plane reappears a little further on when Sasha decides to look for a different room in a different hotel. The project carries with it an orientation towards a future that would be entirely changed, and which is presented in the language of destiny and prophecy:

> I shall exist on a different plane at once if I can get this room, if only for a couple of nights. It will be an omen. Who says you can't escape from your fate? I'll escape from mine, into room number 219.
>
> (37)

But the magical promise of '219', already cast in the form of a knowingly desperate hope, a future orientation for the sake of having an orientation at all, is dissipated without even the room itself, which is occupied, or may be, being shown to be really disappointing, since it is never seen. The narrator reverts from the exaggeration of a counter-fatalistic language to the bitter repetition of the stock phrases of the publicity brochure:[7]

> A beautiful room with a bath? A room with bath? A nice room? A room? . . . But never tell the truth about rooms, because it would bust the roof off everything and undermine the whole social system. All rooms are the same. All rooms have four walls, a door, a window or two, a bed, a chair and perhaps a bidet. A room is a place where you hide from the wolves outside and that's all any room is. Why should I worry about changing my room?
>
> (38)

The specifiable features of 'all rooms' mark off the bare essentials of what is always 'on the same plane' as a shelter from an exterior named in a very different language as 'the wolves' or the threat of a roof catastrophically toppling over the sedate quarters it covered. For in this novel, the demand not to put everything on the same plane is consistently asserted in the opposite form: to ensure a bare minimum of survival – to be 'safe' or 'sane', in the words that keep recurring – it is necessary constantly and deliberately to put everything on the same plane:

> You are walking along a road peacefully. You trip. You fall into blackness. That's the past – or perhaps the future. And

you know there is no past, no future, there is only this
blackness, changing faintly, slowly, but always the same.

(172)

In this paragraph, isolated in the text between a question and
an answer, space and time each merge into an undifferentiated
state, and the peaceful walk is a distant fantasy. The black hole
has neither ground nor time, and after the fall there can only be
a semblance of the missing co-ordinates, superimposed as the
arbitrariness of the plan.

According to the plan, there is a limited set of modifiable
variables to be organised in terms of their own secure sameness. Rooms, streets, persons must all be subject to the
levelling structure of a plan, 'le même plan', in the form of a
daily agenda designed to remove any risk of the unforeseen. As
far as possible, nothing should happen, each day should pass
according to a prearranged programme. Beginning with the
plan itself, we might look at some of these components, one by
one, in no particular order since they are all at the same level,
the same plane.

TO HAVE A PLAN

The plan is introduced from the very beginning, right after the
impasse:

What they call an impasse.
   I have been here five days. I have decided on a place to eat
in at midday, a place to eat in at night, a place to have my
drink in after dinner. I have arranged my little life.

(9)

'My little life' is made up of a repeated sequence of routine
consumption – time to be used up, food and drink to be taken
in, places in which to purchase the right to spend the time to be
passed – and brought into existence through the verbs of
decision and ordering. The narrative thus sets off in the mode
of a future that is already dead, produced in the form of
automatic repetition ('I have . . . I have . . . I have'; 'a place . . . a
place . . . a place'), conceivable only insofar as it must already
have happened, passed without incident.

The assertion of the plan recurs constantly. For instance:

Planning it all out. Eating. A movie. Eating again. One

drink. A long walk back to the hotel. Bed. Luminal. Sleep.
Just sleep – no dreams.

(16)

No complete sentences here, just the bare list in which planning
itself becomes part of the plan:

> What about the programme for this afternoon? That's the
> thing – to have a plan and stick to it. First one thing and then
> another, and it'll all be over before you know where you are.

(52-3)

Planning for plans takes the form of advance consumption of
fixed quantities of time, to be endured rather than enjoyed. The
language is colloquial, pseudo-jolly in its presentation of the
sensible advice which is both adopted and treated as no more
than a minimal protection. Movies and sleep and dinner and
walking are all on the same plane, items on the agenda for
keeping the wolf daily at bay, one after another. 'First one thing
and then another' makes the layout of time, for the day as for
the novel, a matter of sequence without development or cause.
'It'll all be over' means only that there will be no further
demand for a plan. The aim is to come to an end, but also to
stave off the end by the interposition of the plan.

Precise quantities may be calculated, in time and money.
Fours, especially four hundred, keep turning up. Sasha's pay
when she worked for the dress shop is four hundred a month.
The dress they were holding back for her would have cost four
hundred francs. Later, she makes plans for four o'clock – her
date with one of the Russians, her meeting with the other to go
and visit his painter friend, her appointment to have her hair
dyed. For her last date with René, she calculates there will be
four hundred francs left after paying for the hotel and her new
dress. And the book, divided into four parts, is also on this
plane. The endless fours suggest the arbitrary sameness of
planning and recounting levelled out to mere counting, mere
sequence.

Sasha's daily life as a tourist whose time is entirely her own is
translated into the form of the prescribed timetable of the
office or factory worker going through a regular standardised
sequence. Putting these two modes on the same plan or plane
ruins the comfortable differentiation according to which the

two are diametrically opposed, pleasure on one side and obligation on the other, time that is yours to spend and time that does not belong to you. Sasha's extreme case, abolishing the difference by treating leisure as time to be managed, transforms freedom into the terror of a loss of control or an unforeseen incursion from the outside. The plan is a defence and it is all there is.

IDENTITIES

Eat. Drink. Walk. March. Back to the hotel. To the Hotel of Arrival, the Hotel of Departure, the Hotel of the Future, the Hotel of Martinique and the Universe. . . . Back to the hotel without a name in the street without a name. You press the button and the door opens. This is the Hotel Without-a-Name in the Street Without-a-Name, and the clients have no names, no faces. You go up the stairs. Always the same stairs, always the same room.

The room says: 'Quite like old times. Yes? . . . No? . . . Yes.'

(144 – 5)

Rooms, hotels, streets are identical in their nameless standardisation. You find the same room, the same hotel, everywhere – and automatically, at the touch of a button. There are simply two directions, out of and back into the rooms in the hotels which are always the same ones.

Personal identities in the novel are as negative, literally, as those of hotels and streets. They are non-identities, without-identities:

I have no pride – no pride, no name, no face, no country. I don't belong anywhere.

(44)

Pride, name, face, country are there in their absence, formally stated as the separate features of what is not named or identified as the missing person. The four unfulfilled categories recall the four co-ordinates of the daily agenda ('Eat. Drink. Walk. March.'): it is the same kind of list, the same plan. Sasha's husband's name is, was, something entirely indeterminate in its provenance, and there is no mention of any life earlier than their time together either for him or for her. 'Enno' for the man who left her also suggests a brutal literalisation of such denials, legal and personal, N-O, one letter at a time.

This sort of negative identity applies to every character encountered in the present time of the novel, and to almost all those who figure in Sasha's memories. The city is peopled almost entirely by foreigners, non-French, but foreignness does not imply a diversity that might be linked to specifiable places of origin. The situation is not one of exile, for these characters never had a home country, or at least the question hardly seems to arise. National identities and names instead become part of a set of signs to be interpreted, personal co-ordinates available for deciphering, without there being any reason to suppose that they correspond to a truth, of origin or of legal fact. Names, when proffered, are of indeterminate origin, their plausibility or otherwise forming part of the jousting process between the newly met in the city (was René, if that is his name, really in the Foreign Legion? Are the Russians really Russians?).

There is no distinction between genuine and faked identity. It is only a question of formalities. Sasha's reassurance at having a ticket to sit in the Luxembourg Gardens, making 'everything legal' (53) is on the same plane as the bungled identity slip for the hotel:

> What's wrong with the fiche? I've filled it up all right, haven't I? Name So-and-so, nationality So-and-so. . . . Nationality – that's what has puzzled him. I ought to have put nationality by marriage.
>
> (14)

Even officially, nationality and name are matters of convention, subject to alteration. Sasha's first name is not the one she was first given:

> Was it in 1923 or 1924 that we lived round the corner, in the Rue Victor-Cousin, and Enno bought me that Cossack cap and the imitation astrakhan coat? It was then that I started calling myself Sasha. I thought it might change my luck if I changed my name.
>
> (12)

The adoption of a new identity, connoting a different country of origin, derives from nothing more than a superstitious whim. The clothes bought in Paris are Russian or fake Russian (who knows if the Cossack cap is 'imitation' like the coat?), and their indeterminate identity rather reinforces than pre-empts Sasha's own appellation by a different label. Following, or alongside this Russian or quasi-Russian first name, there is a surname, Jansen, also acquired by proxy (it is presumably Enno's, but this is never stated). Yet at the same time, with these two names, Sasha does not say no to the designation 'Anglaise' which is several times applied to her, in actual utterances or in her projection of them. Most comically amid all the random permutations of names and nationalities, there appears one figure of certain country:

> He has a friend called Dickson, A Frenchman, who sings at the Scala. He calls himself Dickson because English singers are popular at the moment.
>
> (115)

Like any other marketable item, names can be put on or off according to vagaries of fashion or fantasy.

A French inhabitant of Paris passes himself off as an Anglais, and there is no suggestion that one city's identity is significantly different from that of any other. Like streets, rooms and hotels, cities are all the same. Sasha seems to have been in London, Amsterdam, Brussels, but it is not said where her movements started or why. There is little to distinguish the places except for the occasional specification of a street or family name with a local connotation. For the most part, cities contain the same mixture of foreign names, true or not to the geographical starting point of their bearers.

National identities, legal and linguistic, can also be bought and sold, changed or exchanged for something other than superstitions or fashions in coats or names. René wants, or purports to want, a forged passport. Sasha, when pregnant, gave English lessons. The novel's own writing jumbles fragments from several languages, in the text as well as in the names. They are not translated. This has the effect of putting them all on the same plane, undifferentiated, but also of disconnecting, breaking up whatever sense the basic English of the narrative might be making. When Sasha lost her job at the dress shop it was because she did not appear to the visiting English owner – non-name, 'Mr. Blank' – to be the fluent speaker of French and German for which the Italian manager had taken her when he hired her. But there is no test before or after. One day she passed off as someone speaking several languages, today she doesn't. It is not a matter of qualifications corresponding to measurable skills, but of looking as though you possess them, or someone being disposed to see you as possessing them.

MIRRORS, CLOTHES AND MONEY

A new dress, like a new room, can act as a temporary promise of a total change. But its disappointment is written into the very expression of the wish. Sasha's desired dress is introduced at the very point when she is no longer going to have it because she is being sacked:

> In this fitting-room there is a dress in one of the cupboards which has been worn a lot by the mannequins and is going to be sold off for four hundred francs. The saleswoman has promised to keep it for me. I have tried it on; I have seen myself in it. It is a black dress with wide sleeves embroidered in vivid colours – red, green, blue, purple. It is my dress. If I had been wearing it I should never have stammered or been stupid.

> (28)

'I have seen myself in it.' The mirror elided here makes up the identity otherwise lacking. In this dress she has *seen* herself, and also seen *herself*, the two for once fitting together. This perfect creation of a competent, sure self is remembered at the point at which it has already been lost, has ceased to be posed as a possibility. It is no more than the memory of what was only ever an anticipation.

One of the deliberately fabricated parts of Sasha's plan for her two weeks in Paris, this one extending over the whole period, is the 'transformation act' (63). This consists of the purchase of a new dress and new hat, and in having her hair dyed platinum blond. Rather than a cumulative construction or reconstruction, this project is one of spending for its own sake, without regard for the object. In this sense it is like the other forms of consumption or prospective consumption laid out in a plan for the day:

Tomorrow I'll go to the Galeries Lafayette, choose a dress, go along to the Printemps, buy gloves, buy scent, buy lipstick, buy things costing fcs. 6.25 and fcs. 19.50, buy anything cheap. Just the sensation of spending, that's the point. I'll look at bracelets studded with artificial jewels, red, green and blue, necklaces of imitation pearls, cigarette-cases, jewelled tortoises. . . . And when I have had a couple of drinks I shan't know whether it's yesterday, today, or tomorrow.

(145)

Tomorrow is represented today as the time when the difference between them will have been abolished through what is already laid out as a progressive reduction in organised deliberation. First there is or will be the two stores, the dress and the accessories to accompany it, the modestly priced purchasable goods. 'Just the sensation of spending' then turns into a random list of commodities marked by their absurdity or artificiality, just to be looked at, and finally becomes the vagueness of 'a couple of drinks', not exactly as planned but 'when I have had', something that will have happened.

The promise of the new image is thwarted before it has begun, a chance of changing which is already written out as a future failure. The same bind governs the whole enterprise of buying a new persona. At first, it is partly to counteract the charge of looking old that she hears coming from the outside, in the voice of the man in the café who refers to her as 'la vieille' (41). Fiercely rejected at first, this identity is then taken on as her own. In another café, overhearing another remark about her, Sasha adds 'la vieille' herself when she mutters the sentence over afterwards (50, 54).

One one side, then, there is the desire not so much to be, as to look beautiful. On the other is the practical difficulty of appearing to be wealthy. The better your outfit, the more you will be accosted by gigolos who want your money. Because Sasha wears a fur coat, she seems to have more than she has. Wanting to look neither old nor rich, she has no way out. This is what appears in the dream of the London underground and the Exhibition:

Everywhere there are placards printed in red letters: This Way to the Exhibition, This Way to the Exhibition. But I don't want the way to the exhibition – I want the way out. There are passages to the right and passages to the left, but no exit sign. Everywhere the fingers point and the placards read: This Way to the Exhibition. . . .

(13)

This impasse, with the exit blocked, forces you to enter the show, to make a spectacle of yourself. Sasha's encounters with men will all turn around a question of who is exhibiting what to whom, who is the buyer and who is the seller. So René shows off his teeth (and is embarrassed when Sasha recognises the gesture as showing off, not smiling).

It is taken for granted that exchanges will take place according to evaluations and calculations which will include money as one of their principal currencies, but can also convert everything else to this form:

But there you are, when you're determined to get people on the cheap, you shouldn't be surprised when they pitch you their own little story of misery sometimes.

(90)

The positions alternate between that of the buyer on a budget and the advertiser with a negative line. The little story of misery may or may not correspond to something true; all that counts is its credibility, its ability to convince the other that the lack falls more on your side.

But for the woman the sign of age adds another layer of complication. Age accompanied by the wealth signified by the fur coat means you will be taken to want to pay for the services of a gigolo; age not accompanied by the signs of wealth means you are without a recognisable public place: 'Qu'est-ce qu'elle fout ici, la vieille?', 'What is the old woman doing here?', in the phrase that repeats and repeats in Sasha's head. Whence the projection all the time onto others of dismissive evaluations:

'A Pernod,' I say to the waiter.
He looks at me in a sly, amused way when he brings it.
God, it's funny being a woman! And the other one – the one behind the bar – is she going to giggle or to say something about me in a voice loud enough for me to hear? That's the way she's feeling.
No, she says nothing. . . . But she says it all.

(104)

It makes no difference whether anyone actually speaks. Voices real or imagined 'say something about me'.

Mirrors work in the same way, as nothing but negative confirmation. The only moment when the mirror makes a promise rather than marking a decline is the already frustrated, long-past incident of the new dress that never materialised. Like rooms and streets and other people, mirrors deliver disparaging, snide assessments:

> This is another lavatory that I know very well, another of the well-known mirrors.
>
> 'Well, well,' it says, 'last time you looked in here you were a bit different, weren't you? Would you believe me that, of all the faces I see, I remember each one, that I keep a ghost to throw back at each one – lightly, like an echo – when it looks into me again? All glasses in all lavabos do this.'
>
> (170)

The mirror is separated off as a sneer apart from the image, a third person always present along with the face-to-face of the woman looking and her image.

There are no scenes of men looking in mirrors in the novel, but there are scenes where the woman's looking is overlooked. Sasha remembers the bald woman happily trying on hats when she was working in the dress shop, and her daughter seeking to establish a cruel complicity (22). This time in Paris, at a double remove, she is transfixed as she looks unseen through a shop window at a grotesque figure:

> There is a customer inside. Her hair, half-dyed, half-grey, is very dishevelled. As I watch she puts on a hat, makes a face at herself in the glass, and takes it off very quickly. She tries another – then another. Her expression is terrible – hungry, despairing, hopeful, quite crazy. At any moment you expect her to start laughing the laugh of the mad.
>
> I stand outside, watching. I can't move. Hat after hat she puts on, makes that face at herself in the glass and throws it off again. Watching her, am I watching myself as I shall become?
>
> (68)

Though she stands apart, Sasha looks on the other woman as though she were her own image. She is unable to leave the exhibition, although it is not her on show. A negative image is seen as her future, a good image can only be what the mirror throws mockingly back from the past.

OLD TIMES

The mirror is not seen to repair or improve what has always been irrevocably lost. One memory pinpoints a beginning to this at the moment when Enno left:

> Did I love Enno in the end? Did he ever love me? I don't know. Only, it was after that that I began to go to pieces.
>
> (143)

But despite the attempt to mark a time when she had not yet gone 'to pieces', the memories of the time with Enno are only slightly or occasionally happier than those of the subsequent times. There is a pleasure in their getting to Paris and finding a room (124), there is Lise, the friend she loves. But the hopes are always slightly fantastic, in proportion to the lack of money, the drift from one city and country to another, vaguely seeking for something else. There is no time before they were together, but equally, there seems to be no reason why they were together. Old times, when Sasha was young or younger, or might have been, come in not so much as distinct and separate as in their menace to the fragile state of constructed survival. Sasha pieced together cannot live with a Sasha who might never have broken apart; for the present to be tolerable, there must never have been a choice, never a future.

So memory operates in echoes and doublings, as a continuous present. It is triggered by the recognition of a place, dissociating here now from here then, or the lash of a remark that identifies her as an old woman – 'Tu la connais, la vieille?' (41) – and which leads not to the evocation of a happier youth, but to a memory of a wish for her death attributed to others as well as to herself. It may also be prompted by hearing the same piece of music (the streets of Good Morning, Midnight are streets of songs as much as streets of sights):

> Walking to the music of L'Arlésienne, remembering the coat I wore then – a black-and-white check with big pockets.
>
> (86)

The memory then takes over the narrative and it requires the repetition of the same phrase to initiate the recall to the here and now:

Walking to the music of *L'Arlésienne*. . . . I feel for the pockets of the check coat, and I am surprised when I touch the fur of the one I am wearing. . . . Pull yourself together, dearie. This is late October, 1937, and that old coat had its last outing a long time ago.

(91)

There is no difference in style between present and past times, and both will appear in the present tense. This is not a narrator who looks back on her youth with the maturity of experience, as a different person. She has to piece or pull herself together to fit the present which is only marked off by the arbitrariness of a precise date and the physical evidence of a different coat.

Stories with happy endings have their place somewhere else, in the privileged sentimental creations of the rich woman by whom Sasha was once employed as secretary to her dictations. Distinctions are blurred not only between past and present, or between beginnings and endings. For it may also be impossible to say whether the flashes or flashbacks elicited alongside the present time are memories or daydreams. This passage follows from Sasha asking René to whistle her a particular melody:

I am in a little whitewashed room. The sun is hot outside. A man is standing with his back to me, whistling that tune and cleaning his shoes. I am wearing a black dress, very short, and heel-less slippers. My legs are bare. I am watching for the expression on the man's face when he turns round. Now he ill-treats me, now he betrays me. He often brings home other women and I have to wait on them, and I don't like that. But as long as he is alive and near me I am not unhappy. If he were to die I should kill myself.
My film-mind. . . . ('For God's sake watch out for your film-mind. . . .')

(176)

Though details in this – the black dress, the man who brings another woman home – are recognisable as possible memories, given what has already been said of Sasha's past, there is no way of being sure that this is to be understood as memory rather than fiction. It reveals another levelling process, in the impossibility of distinguishing between a memory that might really have happened and a fantasy that hasn't. The drift of 'my film-mind' picks up pieces from what is remembered, and the past will be pulled together from elements that are already familiar in terms of the present story. This fantasy or memory is fully part of the present in which it returns or shows itself, continuing the narrative in exactly the same mode. Only the parenthetical effort of self-censure – '(("For God's sake watch out")' – restores the semblance of a separation between 'late October, 1937' – this street, this man – and its analogues in memory or imagination.

At the end, when René has left the hotel room, there is an explicit division into two selves, one resembling the voice of censuring sanity and turning into a cynical transformer of the other's life into corny catchlines:

> Her voice in my head: 'Well, well, just think of that now. What an amusing ten days! Positively packed with thrills. The last performance of What's-her-name And Her Boys or It Was All Due To An Old Fur Coat. Positively the last performance. . . . Go on, cry, allez-y.'
>
> (184 – 5)

The mocking onlooker here is internalised as part of the narrator herself, bitchily satirising the past as a series of identically predictable shows. But the 'film-mind' suggests not only the distraction of sensational stories, but also something else which works constantly to break both past and present times into a looker and her image, while the exhibition remains the same:

> They finish their vermouth and go out and I sit alone in a large, clean, empty room and watch myself in the long glass opposite, turning over the pages of an old number of l'Illustration, thinking that I haven't got a care in the world, except that tomorrow's Sunday – a difficult day anywhere. Sombre dimanche. . . .
> Planning it all out. Eating. A movie.
>
> (16)

'Turning over the pages' could refer either to Sasha or to the image she is watching. She is always doubled, without the one outside the mirror being more real than the other.

In the case of a division between times, Sasha in the present is spectator to the movie of Sasha then:

> The gramophone record is going strong in my head: 'Here this happened, here that happened. . . .'
> I used to work in a shop just off this street.
> I can see myself coming out of the Métro station at the Rond-Point every morning at half-past eight . . .
> (17; second ellipsis added)

This occurs just after Sasha has been to the cinema, watching the same film through twice. Exact repetition, as if 'according to programme' (16), makes a parody of the carefully ordered plan for the day, and leads to another form of mechanical replay. The mental gramophone record turns as the automatic repetition of past events (there will follow a long section of scenes from the shop and the day she was given the sack), with this narrator placing herself not in direct identification but as the one who sees Sasha then coming out of the métro and going to work, day after day. The younger times of the old times insist on showing themselves once more, the same old picture, but watched at a distance.

The mechanical smoothness of the past as film or gramophone record, identically reproduced, is one more mode of the attempted production of a seamless, fault-free model, according to a plan, 'no gaps' (15). As with the transformation after the birth of the baby, such a state is equivalent in its perfection and changelessness to death, or to the lifeless motion of the machine. The present is already perceived in the separation of its registration, according to plan, verifiable in the mirror. Sasha compares herself to an automaton (10) and in the dress shop she animates the dummies, 'those damned dolls, thinking what a success they would have made of their lives if they had been women' (18). The models exhibit a woman's appearance as fashion, something to be bought, and by the same logic a living woman is measured by the standard of a walking commodity, 'not quite so good as new' (93).

The artifice of the machine and its analogues is set, like the plan for a smooth routine, against a monstrosity it barely conceals:

> All that is left in the world is an enormous machine,

made of white steel. It has innumerable flexible arms, made
of steel. Long, thin arms. At the end of each arm is an eye,
the eyelashes stiff with mascara.

(187)

This is the new dawn, nightmare image of *Good Morning,
Midnight*, world-body out of joint, in pieces as pure machine, but
a machine which has no recognisable order, with its numberless
eyes, stiffened into a stare, protruding or grasping where they
take the place of hands. The viewer is watched, apprehended,
by the glaring unidentifiable spectatorness which is all over,
and all over her. But the looking thing is also an image of Sasha
herself, a defensive machine gone 'to pieces' out of all relation,
endlessly making itself up with endless additions, steel and
mascara for the platinum blond hair she acquires as part of her
'transformation act'.

ROOMS OF ONE'S OWN

The title *Good Morning, Midnight*, has the effect of situating the
novel as part of a tradition of women's writing in a mode of
antithetical, negative irony. Emily Dickinson's poem, the source
of the title, is quoted in full as an epigraph, and seems to
prepare from the outset, as a plan which will not be abandoned,
for a world which will present new days or new beginnings
only in the form of impossibility, as the bitter allusion to a long-
lost promise which now figures only in its inaccessibility
('Sunshine was a sweet place, / I liked to stay – /But Morn didn't
want me – now – / So good night, Day!').

But Rhys's novel also suggests the comparison with Woolf,
who was her contemporary. Woolf's famous demand for five
hundred pounds a year and a room of her own as the basis for a
woman's independence is almost literally answered in the
situation of Rhys's Sasha. In the same almost magical way as
for Woolf's Mary Carmichael, the income appears through the
unexpected legacy of a female relative. It is rather more modest
than Mary Carmichael's five hundred, but in the same way it
provides for living expenses. This much similarity makes way
for the irony:

Well, that was the end of me, the real end. Two-pound-ten
every Tuesday and a room off the Gray's Inn Road. Saved,

rescued and with my place to hide in – what more did I want? I crept in and hid. The lid of the coffin shut down with a bang. Now I no longer wish to be loved, beautiful, happy or successful. I want one thing and one thing only – to be left alone.

(42–3)

Instead of providing the material basis for a fuller life, as in Woolf's fantasy, the room and income here close everything out. Sasha has just uttered a diatribe against the world of 'them' as cliché:

They think in terms of a sentimental ballad. And that's what terrifies you about them. It isn't their cruelty, it isn't even their shrewdness – it's their extraordinary naiveté. Everything in their whole bloody world is a cliché. Everything is born out of a cliché, rests on a cliché, survives by a cliché. And they believe in the clichés – there's no hope.

(42)

'Loved, beautiful, happy or successful' lists the world now shut off as a set of clichés; life, outside the 'coffin' of the room, is also a death, mechanical repetition. Once more – 'good morning, midnight' – the opposite terms are equated, and the positive one represented only in the irony of its foreordained unattainability.

So Woolf's private room becomes in Rhys either a coffin or one of an infinitely repeatable series, and *Mrs Dalloway*, Woolf's novel about a middle-aged woman walking around in the modern city, looks like a sentimental ballad in comparison with the negative *flâneuse* of *Good Morning, Midnight*. In *Mrs Dalloway*, there are clear differentiations between past and present; what was potential but unfulfilled in Clarissa's life may return, but it is never on the same plane as the present day. Clarissa can enjoy the life of this particular day – in June 1923 – as marked off from every other; in *Good Morning, Midnight*, the specification of 'late October, 1937' functions as a sharp and arbitrary recall to a reality which is always drifting off.

The comparisons can be continued. In both novels, there is a perpetual movement into memory and daydream. In the first-person narrative of *Good Morning, Midnight* this happens only in relation to Sasha herself, and it often takes the form of a total removal from the present situation, so that she must be drawn back from her absence by the feel of a different coat pocket, or the laugh out loud which confuses her companion. The memory, in other words, takes over and has no more or less reality than the present, to which it has no relation of difference. These lapses of distraction make 'gaps' in the present, but the present is defined in the first place as simply that which is subject to the plan for the avoidance of gaps.

In *Mrs Dalloway*, lines going backwards and forwards between different periods of life and different moments of relationships structure the narrative with all the precision that then makes this one day not just any day. Except with Septimus Smith, the movement of thoughts to other places and other times does not imply the removal of attention from the present on which the past impinges, but only in such a way that the difference between the two is still maintained. Characters have backgrounds and histories known to themselves and to others who know them, including the narrator, and these are clearly connected to cultural as well as private events.

But in *Good Morning, Midnight*, Septimus's schizophrenic dislocation is closer to a norm in Sasha's mental and social universe. There are no relations of origin or orientation between different times and characters; for the most part connections consist in tenuous encounters in capital cities, forming and breaking for no particular reason. The collapse of one period into another applies to historical as well as personal times. In this much more cosmopolitan world of temporary encounters always overlaid by implicit negotiations around sex and money, there is no bearing to a story outside its plausibility in the immediate situation:

> We stop under a lamp-post to guess nationalities. So they say, though I expect it is because they want to have a closer look at me.

(46)

In a memory of the early twenties, 'this after-war generation' appears in the form of a cliché – they are 'mad for pleasure', in a repeated phrase (89) – put into the mouth of a man who briefly picks Sasha up and misinterprets her tottering, rapidly drunk from lack of food, as a sign that she wants to dance. Just once, in a moment as lacking in detail as Sasha's allusion to her family when she receives the news of her legacy, there is a question about the relation of Enno's lack of money and the war:

> He was a chansonnier, it seems, before he became a journalist. He enlisted during the first week of the war. From 1917 onwards a gap. He seemed very prosperous when I met him in London, but now no money – nix. What happened? He doesn't tell me.
>
> (114)

This admission of a 'gap' occurs in the context of the fullest history of any character in this novel, not excluding the heroine. Normally, everything is kept on the deliberate plane of no questions asked and the gaps not even suggested.

While the regular chiming of Big Ben in Woolf's novel marks a symbolic framework which is the context for, but does not exclude other kinds of timing which work in different ways, for Rhys the daily plan is a be-all stressed as an end-all, a programme for life as the death of carrying out a faultless routine. Clarissa is by no means as unequivocally 'positive' as she appears in the eyes of a fatuous admirer: she has her moment of paranoia when confronted by the figure of her daughter's governess, and her belief in 'life' is set against a constant threat of disintegration. But in this novel the world as menace and the self in pieces are represented not by her but by Septimus Smith. The negative elements are not lacking in *Mrs Dalloway*, either for the central character or for the world in which she moves, but the affirmation against them is not struck with the line of impossibility that constantly marks the movements of Rhys's Sasha. Ironically, Sasha's self-programming resembles the psychiatrist's prescription for 'Proportion' in Septimus's life that is the object of such sharp criticism in Woolf's novel.

Sasha's film-mind imagines other kinds of story, too, including one that is categorically impossible. This appears in the middle of a conversation between Sasha and René, between a question and an answer in a paragraph which, like other daydreams and memories, departs from the present without any demarcation:

> 'I'm no use to anybody,' I say. 'I'm a cérébrale, can't you see that?'
> Thinking how funny a book would be, called 'Just a

Cérébrale or You Can't Stop Me From Dreaming'. Only, of course, to be accepted as authentic, to carry any conviction, it would have to be written by a man. What a pity, what a pity!

'Is that your idea of yourself?' he says.

(161)

To him, 'cérébrale' means a 'monster' (162) of narcissistic self-containment, uninterested in either sex, to her an intelligent or dreaming woman, so the lack of conviction starts right in the middle of things, between the two utterances, since the man and woman do not even see eye to eye about whose story it is which might be told, by whichever sex. This impasse places them in positions that are not only different in relation to one another, but entail incompatible fantasies of what a woman might be, with or without a story.

Elsewhere in the book, the painter's telling of the story told him in London by the woman from Martinique puts this issue in another way. For one thing, the Martinique woman is insulted where she lives not because of her sex but because of her race. Later on, when René is boasting about his prospects in London and thinks Sasha's doubts about it are because 'everybody knows England isn't a woman's country' (157):

That's his idea. But he'll find out that he will be up against racial, not sexual, characteristics.

(157)

And secondly, the Martinique woman's story is put into the mouth of a man, which would seem ironically to reinforce the assertion that it is only the male narrator who carries authority. But his story, including the woman's story that he tells, is in turn reported only within the pages of a novel by a woman. The layers of ironic ventriloquism do not stop here, for this is a novel written by a woman who is herself from the Caribbean – and who, almost thirty years later, would write the supplement to *Jane Eyre* which tells the story of Rochester's West Indian wife, Bertha Mason. In the context of *Wide Sargasso Sea*, Sasha's name changes[8] and the mad laughter of *Good Morning, Midnight* may look like a first version of the later story, in the same way that *Jane Eyre* reread by *Wide Sargasso Sea* appears in a different light.

IMPASSION

In rhetoric, an 'impasse' defines a structure where the proposition includes assumptions which are contrary to those of the addressee, who is thus unable either to reply according to the same terms, or to deny something on which s/he has not been directly challenged.[9] 'Did Jean Rhys's comic view of life attract you?' implies a certain interpretation of her novels.

Good Morning, Midnight takes the impasse as one of its themes: there is no way out, the street is an impasse. But it is structured like a rhetorical impasse too, since all its positive terms are already excluded with the force of impossibility (once there might have been hope for change, for a long time there has been none). As an impasse, and as the story of an impasse, the novel does not pretend to go very far. But as a woman's story written by a woman, it claims with ironic precision to be unconvincing.

NOTES

1 *Wide Sargasso Sea* (1966), Rhys's rewriting of *Jane Eyre* from the point of view of Bertha Mason and others, is quite different in this respect. Its return to an earlier novel at the time may also, however - as I shall suggest later on - provide a way of imagining how to reread the prewar novels now.
2 Suggestive accounts from this point of view are to be found in Judith Kegan Gardiner, 'Good Morning, Midnight; Good Night Modernism', *boundary 2*, 11 (Fall/Winter 1982-3), pp. 233-51 and Molly Hite, 'Writing in the margins: Jean Rhys' in *The Other Side of the Story: Structures and Strategies of Contemporary Feminist Narrative* (Ithaca: Cornell University Press, 1989), pp. 19-54, and Deborah Kelly Kloepfer, *The Unspeakable Mother: Forbidden Discourse in Jean Rhys and H.D.* (Ithaca: Cornell University Press, 1989), especially chapter 5. All three in different ways seek to shift a burden of causation onto social forms that produce the warps from which women suffer. For Hite, this is crucially a sexualised operation. It is as women that women both experience and cannot get free from a psychic pain inflicted by a sexist commodity society: 'Rhys's protagonists are victims who are fully aware of their victimization' (p. 28). For Gardiner, the trouble is equally social and historical, but less exclusively harmful towards women: 'She shows that bourgeois polarizations of experience induce a passive despair compliant to the *status quo* as midnight descends on Europe' (p. 234). Kloepfer, looking from the other direction, sees some glimmer of feminine hope in her marking of positive, pre-Oedipal forms of language

enjoyed by mother and child before the onset of paternal social constraints, and retrievable through Sasha's linguistic looseness and her memories of childbirth. For a reading which does not attempt to read Rhys through any single determination, see Sue Roe, ' "The Shadow of Light": The Symbolic Underworld of Jean Rhys' in Roe (ed.), *Women Reading Women Writing* (Brighton: Harvester, 1987), pp. 229–64.

3 Jean Rhys, *Good Morning, Midnight* (1938; rpt. New York: Harper & Row, 1982), p. 9. Subsequent quotations will be included within the text. Ellipses, unless otherwise stated, are Rhys's not mine.

4 A feature also remarked by Elizabeth Abel in 'Women and Schizophrenia: The Fiction of Jean Rhys', *Contemporary Literature*, vol. 20 (Spring 1979), p.164.

5 In her biography of Rhys, Carole Angier says of Sasha that 'Her attempt at motherhood is a tragedy, but everything else is a farce' (*Jean Rhys: Life and Work*, London: André Deutsch, 1990, p. 379). However, it is not clear that the birth itself, as reported from the present perspective, is to be understood any less farcically than its returns and analogues. The 'tragedy' of *Good Morning, Midnight* might have to do with just this impossibility of making distinctions between different orders of experience: there is nothing before the farce of repetition.

6 The first name of the writer whose pen-name was Colette, who may thus be being pointed out here as more positive in her outlook than the present woman writer about women and love in Paris.

7 *After Leaving Mr Mackenzie* (1930) reproduces a hotel's publicity card on the very first page.

8 In addition to her own adoption of Sasha, there is the store manager who insists on calling her Sophia (p. 42).

9 See for instance Bernard Dupriez, *Gradus: Les procédés littéraires (Dictionnaire)* (1984; rpt. Paris: Christian Bourgois, 10/18 collection, 1991), p. 248.

Chapter 3

p/s: the return of *m/f*

The figure of the *passante* as she appears in Baudelaire and then in Proust has taken us along a number of subsequent streets, in Paris and elsewhere, which now turn out to be walked by women who have other representations to make. With all the differences between them, both Rhys and Woolf bring into sharp focus the difficulty of moving away from a story that seems to have structured the sexual scene once and for all. In this chapter, we look not so much at the displacements implied or attempted in literary ways, as at the possible moves to be made through another kind of feminist writing: that of a theoretical journal.

m/f – subtitled 'a feminist journal' – was published in ten issues that appeared between 1978 and 1986, when the final number both nobly and mournfully declared itself on the cover as 'The Last Issue'. In 1990, *October* books published an anthology of *m/f* articles, paying tribute to the journal's continuing influence well after the time of its first appearance.[1] This external history itself raises interesting questions about feminist history, and the history of feminist theory. But within its pages too, *m/f* constantly addressed problems of the relation between historically general structures of sexual difference and particular local interventions. Without a discordance between the two, there could be no feminism, and no histories, feminist or otherwise; but the tension between them as modes of analysis also remained unresolved – in ways which could then take us somewhere new again. All these questions, as I try to show, are closely connected to the position of the *passante* in her oddly unstable temporality: as the might-have-been whose doubleness makes way for a history, and the timeless who is situated outside the possibility of any movement. Let us begin with this last.

THE ETERNAL PASSANTE

Seen in her Baudelairean and Proustian lights, the *passante* does not seem at all like a localised figure. And once she has been drawn out in this way, an identification to be projected potentially onto any woman, anywhere, we might take this still further and look at her as a quasi-mythological, timeless figure.

For this scenario contains some familiar elements. First – in the beginning – there is *the* woman, created out of an extra bit added on from and by the man. The rib is removed from Adam to make Eve, beautiful and whole, but formed from a fragment. She is a lost piece of him, the primordial 'complementary part': in the beginning, they were one. But as long as she lives they cannot be reunited, for her very existence depends on their separation.

The Biblical genesis of woman is not the only mythical echo called forth by the *passante*. Baudelaire's, irretrievably lost, is as though dead and gone: in her disappearance, she passes on her loss to the poet. Like the widowed Orpheus, who descends into Hades in quest of Eurydice, he seeks her only in her death. And just as Orpheus can have her back only on condition that he does not look back at her – one glimpse, and she will be gone – so the writing which brings back the *passante* can only follow after a sighting that is never to be repeated.[2]

'THE' WOMAN, *ENCORE*

And if Baudelaire and Proust have said it already, perhaps Lacan says it some more, *encore*. For we seem to have been approaching a point where the *passante* has come to look indistinguishable from the psychoanalytic figure of femininity, in all her fantasmatic ambiguity.

Several features that may be glimpsed in the *Encore* seminars would seem to lend support to at least a partial identification of the Lacanian 'woman' with the *passante*:

> We could in theory write $x R y$, and say that x is the man, y is the woman, and R is the sexual relation. Why not? Only

there's this, it's stupid, because what is supported under the signifying function, of *man* and of *woman*, are only signifiers completely bound up with the current-run (*courcourant*) usage of language. If there is a discourse which demonstrates this to you, it must be psychoanalytic discourse, in making an issue of this, that the woman will never be taken other than *quoad matrem*. The woman only does her job (*entre en fonction*) in the sexual relationship as the mother.[3]

There is no sexual relation, '*Il n'y a pas de rapport sexuel*'. The poet and his *passante* never meet, there is nothing more than what he sees in her. But at the same time, it is the fantasy of their complementarity, their being made for each other, which engenders the endless wish for their unity.

The mother: no getting away from her, but she has always left you. You, the man: from the moment that the mother turns out to be 'a woman' there is no going back, nothing for it but to seek her again, hopelessly, for what now seems to have been the perfect link is broken forever. So – the most usual outcome – 'women', one after the other, all the same in that they are not her, the one and only, but could or should have been, 'O you whom I would have loved!' (You, the woman, a woman, too, from the moment that the mother turns out to be one. A different story, into which the *passante* seen by the poet enters rather as a problem of identification: to be or not to be [like] her.) 'There is not *the* woman, the woman is *not all* [*pas toute*]'.[4] 'The' woman does not exist, the woman as perfect complement, but she is seen as potentially this, as truth, all, from the man's projection. The 'fragmentary' *passante* who *would have been* all is projected as all by what the imagination supplies to her appearance – both in that she is seen as lacking, and that she makes up for a lack in the man.

What leaves some likelihood for what I am putting forward, namely, that of this *jouissance*, the woman knows nothing, is that all the time we've been begging them, begging them on our knees – last time I was talking about women psychoanalysts – to try to tell us, well, not a word! We have never been able to get anything out of them.[5]

Who knows what she wants? Her *jouissance* may be other than phallic, but she won't say or can't. '*O toi qui le savais*', you knew it but you said not a word. 'If the libido is only masculine, the dear woman, it is only from where she is all, which is to say from where the man sees her, from nowhere but there that the dear woman can have an unconscious.'[6] Only masculine libido, phallic organisation of *jouissance* as far as it can be articulated. It is all seen from the masculine side: no desire, no imagining from her side can be represented.

ÇA, A WOMAN

There is more to it than that. Sometimes it seems as if Lacan is also presenting the unconscious itself, and not only the (impossible) woman, as something not unlike a *passante* in one of her aspects:

> Here we find again the rhythmic structure of this opening and shutting of the crack. . . . The evanescent apparition occurs between two points, the start, the finish of this logical time – between that instant of seeing where something is always elided, even lost, of the intuition itself, and that elusive moment when, precisely, the grasp (*saisie*) of the unconscious does not end, where it is always a matter of a deceptive recuperation.[7]

> In my preceding statements, I have been continually stressing the, in a sense, *pulsative* function of the unconscious, the necessity of vanishing which seems to be in a sense inherent to it – all that, for an instant, appears in its crack seeming to be destined, by a sort of preempting, to close up again, the metaphor Freud himself used, to whisk away, to disappear.[8]

Like the *passante* – 'one flash, then darkness' – the unconscious for Lacan is something that no sooner flickers into view than it is gone again. We might dwell for a moment on the striking similarities in the image. First, that is it indeed an image, a *visual* analogy: the unconscious is seen/not seen, appearing/disappearing – despite the fact that psychoanalysis is a practice whose medium is entirely one of words. The vanishing unconscious is also like the *passante* in that it is always ungraspable – in the very moment, the instant, you have it, it closes off again. And yet it is also what the analyst is seeking, endlessly, and by the very fact of its being 'lost', unattainable as such: no 'recuperation' or recovery other than one that is deceptive, false in its appearance. It slips away, tricky and evasive (there are many different words for this: *se dérober, évanouissante, évasif, élusif, élidé*: it is quite an emphatic betrayal or escape). The impossible feminine apparition is not confined to the manifest consideration of sexuality and sexual difference, but seems to have passed or seeped into the depths of the psychoanalytic account of subjectivity, to produce a covertly gendered unconscious. Or overtly: 'Eurydice twice lost, such is the most tangible image we could give, in myth, of what the relationship is of Orpheus the analyst to the unconscious'.[9]

So many representations from the masculine point of view, of the view as masculine: it is as if Lacanian psychoanalysis provided a culmination to the series of *passante* passages, exposing the terms of her (non)existence in all their intractability.

PAS ÇA, NOT THAT

'*Une femme passa*', 'a woman passed', a woman seen from the masculine position; heard in a different way, '*une femme, pas ça*', 'a woman, not *that*', no thank you. And if we hear '*pas ça*' in a different way again, we find the further objection: not the '*ça*', the usual French translation of Freud's 'id': 'not the unconscious', to which femininity sometimes, at moments, seems to be all but assimilated. If it is taken as a critical exposure of the structure rather than an admiring exposition of it, psychoanalysis seems to offer the perfect account of the cul-de-sacs of a femininity that is conceived simply as a projection of masculine desire. But it offers no immediate ways out, no other place, either female or neutral, outside the given patriarchal or phallocentric scene.

Impasse. Where do 'we' – women? feminists? *passantes*? – go from here? No step seems possible. No step: *pas de pas. Pas pas, papa*: only the old patriarchal story. Unless we said no to all that and looked in a different direction altogether. *Pas*: a no that would also be a step? Or a step that would only represent a denial?

THE MODERN *PASSANTE*

The Freudian/Lacanian line treats the woman/*passante* as the masculine fantasy of femininity, but other feminist approaches have taken different directions. For in another sense, the *passante* could be seen not as univeral figure of fantasy, but as a pre-eminently historical figure, a woman of her time.

Looked at in this way, Baudelaire's *passante* comes across almost as a tableau of the experience of modernity. It is an anonymous encounter which takes place apparently in a large, modern city: the street, anything but a neutral background, is the first subject of the poem, and it is an active, shouting milieu where the couple themselves are silent. There is the fleeting, unforeseen event that shocks, and the peculiar temporality (the sighting is retrospectively fixed as *having* happened, irrevocable in that nothing will alter its significance, and also in that it cannot be recovered in its pristine originality, which is represented only in so far as it is past, or passed away).

Proust's version is differently situated. Unlike Baudelaire's *flâneur*, on foot, noises from the street surrounding him, the viewer here is travelling in a vehicle, and the sighting of the *passante* is an effect of his own speed, his own passage. The *passante* can be anywhere at all along the route, in town or the country; Baudelaire's was a particular, urban *passante*. Proust's *passante* in the passage quoted on pages 10–11 is potentially ubiquitous, 'in the city, in the country': another of the *passante* scenes in *A la recherche du temps perdu* concerns the very type of the country girl, a milkmaid, seen from a train. If it is a crucial part of the poet's experience that this woman emerges and disappears in the street, Proust's narrator seems to be no longer restricted to this setting: the *passante* could be any woman, anywhere – or just anything momentarily seen 'as' a passing woman. The train, the vehicle (horse-drawn here, elsewhere in Proust an automobile) expands the reach of the urban sighting, making the country, too, into a possible site for the glimpse in passing of an unknown woman. The landscape (itself an aesthetic metaphor, implying an externally placed spectator) is turned into a passing scene (cinema, the 'moving picture', is on the horizon already). And the vehicle in which the viewer is situated removes him from any sensory contact with the street itself: the scene in which *passantes* appear is a spectacle seen at a safe, and thereby even more untraversable, distance.

Taking this more historical line, two avenues of analysis open up, two feminist turnings. One would treat the *passante* as a distortion, symptomatic of the patriarchal misrepresentation or misrecognition of women in comparison with what they really are. Look again, look at her as she really is, and you will see something very different from what appears from the perspective of the masculine writer. The *passante* or woman is *not that*, not what she has been shown to be, seen through male eyes; instead, whether already or potentially, there are other, more true-to-life women concealed behind this view of her. This line of investigation might then look at the diversity of the women who actually walked the city streets or the country lanes in this period – of different races or social classes, but united by an oppression that subordinates them all as women, and/or which prevents the expression of their underlying femininity.

The second type of historical approach would not compare the *passante* with another, more accurate picture of women masked by her image, but would look instead at the conditions of representation that made it possible for the woman to be seen as a *passante*, and which, by the same token, might preclude the figure of the *flâneur*, the strolling spectator, from being represented as a woman. This approach would not presuppose a different, more realistic identification of the woman as other than a *passante*, but would, rather, explore the different discourses that construct and constrain various modes of identification, not consistently divided along a line of sexual division.

P/S

The *passante*: perhaps the most ancient and the most modern figure for a woman? Perhaps the figure who throws into confusion any easy distinction between the historical and the timeless, between changing conditions and eternal forms; or between the social and the psychic.

The fable of the *passante* I have just recounted and of the separation of psychic and social forms of analysis has been leading up, step by step, to one view of where *m/f* came in. For, looked at with hindsight (a backward glance, or postscript, to which we shall return), *m/f's* questioning of the figure of woman can be seen as having pointed feminist debates not only towards a distinction between psychic and social questions, but also towards the impossibility of leaving them at that. In thinking p/s, the psychic and the social, m/f refused to treat them as either/or alternatives, and at the same time insisted on the need to think each of them through, on its own terms. After this, the *passante* was never going to look the same again; nor were the eyes of the onlooker going to be identifiable simply as those of a man, or indeed of a woman.

The mysteriousness of m/f's name is a promise, or threat, of the disturbances of these categories. In a sense, the name might seem, provocatively, to flaunt the enigma of femininity in person. Some of its possible senses, clearly never meant to be fixed, are mentioned in the interview in the 'Last Issue' given by an m/f now personified by Parveen Adams and Elizabeth Cowie, to a group of Dutch feminists. Male/female, masculine/ feminine seem the most obvious; but mother/father, Marxism/ Feminism, and even Michel Foucault are also raised as possibilities. There is also a hint of s/s, in its Saussurian and Lacanian versions, to suggest a semiotic or psychoanalytic orientation. At any rate, it is clear that m/f is no univocal figure, and no univocally female figure either.

PAS ÇA ENCORE

From the beginning m/f's project consisted of both a questioning of existing theories of feminism, and a building upon possibilities that had recently been opened up: via psychoanalysis (as an aid rather than a hindrance to feminist understanding) and via new methods of historical analysis. The principal target was the essentialism implied by the first of the two historical lines sketched above. *Essentialism* designated any theory or politics presupposing either a biological or a social unity of women: either their bodies or a consistently operating social 'oppression' determines a unified group identity on the basis of which political demands 'for' women can then be made.

m/f countered this with a double move, which involved both the psychical and the second of the historical lines. On the one hand, there was psychoanalysis, and a concept of a psychical reality that was different from social reality and that rendered problematic any simple reading of the political field. At the same time, the psychoanalytic disruption of the categories of masculinity and femininity as readily transposable to actual men and women challenged the justification for feminist

demands in the name of a common identity, whether femininity was seen as the problem (a false identity imposed by
patriarchal culture) or the goal (the chance of being real women
at last), or both.

On the other hand, and against the same monolithic explana-
tions, there was the notion of a multiplicity of sexual differences, set up in different ways according to the different
discourses – the medical and the legal were the most often
mentioned – in which they appeared. This second model, which
was fairly explicitly taken from Foucault, and in particular from
The Archaeology of Knowledge, made it possible to talk about social
questions, but was not directly hooked onto the first. Psychoanalysis gave 'woman' as fantasy, as a construction without any
essential identity based on either biology or ideology. The
Foucauldian model gave 'women' of many kinds, infinitely
proliferated as different discourses set up particular categories,
open to challenge and, by the same token, infinitely mutable.

Both lines were used strategically to unsettle the assumptions of other arguments that relied on unexamined notions of
individual or social identity. Psychoanalysis was also examined
in its own right, and internal arguments within psychoanalytic
theory were presented and discussed on their own terms. The
aim here again was to root out residual elements of biologism
or normativity so that psychoanalysis (and it was a Lacanian
psychoanalysis that predominated) emerged as the theory that
offered the most thorough challenge to any pinning down, by
her body or by social norms, of the identity of woman.

Yet, although psychoanalysis lends itself very well to the
undoing of all easy assimilations of femininity to femaleness,
and of all invocations of a unified identity as one sex or the other,
it does still require the sexual differentiation of bodies as the
material on which the Oedipus complex and castration will have
their effects, even though these effects will not necessarily
follow the usual – anatomically predictable – paths. A girl who
turns out psychically like a heterosexual man is not in the same
situation, socially or psychically, as a boy to whom this occurs.
But because of its anti-essentialist position, *m/f* at first refrained
from emphasising this aspect of psychoanalysis (which came
more to the fore toward the end), preferring rather to concentrate on how psychoanalysis could be used as a means of
criticising the notions of the body implied in other theories.

The separation of psychoanalytic from social concerns seems much less simple in view of the fact that so many manifestly feminist issues cut across these concerns: issues of sexuality and social regulation, of violence against women, abortion, mothering, etc. This was part of the original argument for the pertinence of psychoanalysis to a movement articulating itself through the slogan 'The personal is political'. But given this situation, it would be more difficult to maintain the strict separation of areas with their corresponding forms of analysis (a question that comes up explicitly in the interview published in the last issue). Psychoanalysis was never presented as providing answers or solutions on a political level, or as deciding, either a priori or in particular cases, whether or not different areas of concern should be regarded as provinces for psychic or social investigation, since it would always be a question of both. But nor was the notion of a multiplicity of heterogeneous discourses going to supply a theory or practice of something that could be unified as 'feminism'. This notion did not allow any special rights to a concept of psychical reality either – since in these terms psychoanalysis, from which the concept was derived, could only be considered as one social discourse among others. In practice, psychoanalysis was exempt from treatment as a social discourse like the others, because that would have made it impossible to use it as an account of a psychic reality fundamentally different from social reality.

It was its recognition of the difficulty of femininity and its lack of fixity that made psychoanalysis attractive to feminists; but psychoanalysis did not propose the means to a general resolution or reform (which would be outside its psychical territory), and could not be used as a basis for feminism other than negatively ('woman is not *that*', ' "woman" is a fantasy'). Yet it was not clear that a Foucauldian analysis could yield a feminist politics either. If women were differently specified in different discourses, every response must be local and nothing could unify them all as 'feminist'. But *m/f* – 'a *feminist* journal' – certainly did want to maintain the political force of that word. Thus when Beverley Brown and Parveen Adams raise the question of how in a community of women the wish or choice to have a child can be assessed, they make clear that:

There are no obvious right and wrong positions here. The organisation of these social relations will indeed affect women and mothers and what we are saying is that it has to be worked out from a *feminist*, not an individual point of view.[10]

The emphatic *feminist* has no given content or programme but keeps its place as an opposing argument, here against the 'individual' point of view.

The question of the nature or necessity of feminist groundings is raised directly from the beginning, but especially in the editorial for issue 5/6 and in the final interview of issue 11/12. It may be focused particularly well from the editorial of issue 4:

A further criticism has been that our analysis produces a political problem of the unity of the Women's Movement. Clearly the Women's Movement is not a coherent expression of oppressed womanhood or a universal condition, but itself a system of alliances between groupings of interests of mothers, workers, lesbians, battered wives, etc., and this does produce the problem of the basis for these alliances, a problem already recognized within socialist feminism. Once this is recognized, it is surprising that the very possibility of using the term 'woman' across a range of constructions is itself raised as an insuperable problem unique to *m/f*.[11]

'Mothers, workers, lesbians, battered wives, etc.' – this particular collectivity is almost the exact antithesis of the *passante*, the negative of the fantasy of 'woman'. These women do not flit by, a look but not a word; instead they form a potentially endless line (etc.') walking the social streets, assorted 'interests' with nothing to consolidate their common identity as women.

The fantasies of 'woman' to be analysed in the register of psychical reality; and/or a proliferation of 'women' constructed through various distinct social discourses: this twofold feminist strategy of questioning might now be seen as having been both *m/f*'s contribution and, perhaps, the point at which it left us divided as to how to proceed from there.

A NEW *PASSANTE*?

And what if *m/f* was itself (herself?) a sort of *passante*, who briefly came and went, marking feminism forever in her passing? The final editorial: 'The moment of *m/f*'s project has now passed'.[12] And so, *m/f*, or several *m/f*s, passed, or passed away: for the body it constituted could only be conceived as a whole once the 'Last Issue' had officially heralded its departure from the scene. What impression did she leave? And what impact will she make now, on her reappearance?

But was she, is she, a woman at all? For this doubt as to *m/f*'s sex was surely the greatest disturbance produced by its interrogation of psychic and social categories. If *m/f* as *passante* was not simply, recognisably, a woman, perhaps its effect was to make it impossible to see the *passante* in the same old ways: sexual identifications had undergone a kind of mutation. This is one crucial sense in which *m/f* both recalls the *passante* and complicates her representation: to the extent that *m/f* is a *passante*, it seems to have challenged the grounds on which the *passante* might clearly be seen as the figure of a woman. *m/f* now seems to have represented a turning point, a disruption of the assumed differentiations of male and female places. Not only was the identity of the woman less immediately ascertainable, but the reader as would-be double of the viewer, the theorist, or his/her object was no longer simply assigned to one sex either. For one thing, like feminist writings before, *m/f* had dislocated the ready positionings in taking up the place of the theorist. But this did not mean *m/f* was seeking to identify a woman, or indeed that it identified itself as being simply one or the other.

To all appearances, this disturbance of clearly marked sexual boundaries was the source of much of the criticism of the journal at the time of its first publication, taken up implicitly and explicitly within its pages. How can it be a good move, a valid step, for feminism to put in question the unity of women, the identity of women as a political group? Doesn't this just leave 'us' in the lurch, without a collective, even less an individual, body to grow from or cling to? Without some anchor, some theory of a general oppression of women to steady its passage, is not feminism left adrift amid a sea of floating signifiers? Against which, painstakingly and methodically, *m/f* insisted, over and over again, on the need to distinguish between sexual divisions and sexual differences, a distinction that was related to the problem of how to conceptualise the relations between the social and the psychic, or of how to formulate a 'feminist' politics when the very identity of woman or women was understood as being open to question. The force of the criticisms the journal encountered at the time and subsequently (for it continues to be read and debated), the way it was perceived as going *too far*, is itself some measure of what it did to shake up the set ways of feminist thinking that turned on an already given sexual division. Something was in the process of being changed.

But not in the same ways for everyone. For some who turned away from *m/f* to begin with, seeing in it the grotesque opposite of a positive image of woman, a sort of ugly sister bent on impeding the harmonious progress of feminism, the journal's questions later came to seem important, even inescapable. Here the second look at a figure who could hardly have seemed more repulsive has revealed instead something irresistible that went unremarked in the rapid dismissal of the first glance or first reading.

And then there were those for whom, at the time, *m/f* was like a feminist *passante* in person, a fleeting apparition of something that seemed as if it might be going to answer to every hitherto unarticulated wish for something else. A momentary passing, a last glimpse, and then s/he is gone, 'Fleeting Beauty/Whose look made me suddenly reborn'. *m/f* seemed to breathe new life into feminism, for those of 'us' seeing in 'her' a different and new way of putting the questions, turning or twisting the settled patterns of looking and thinking about where feminism might possibly be going. But if she made her mark then, indelibly and irrevocably, to look at her now 'as she first appeared' would be quite impossible. To the extent that *m/f*'s new questions were taken up, taken in, she became part of feminism, part of us. That means that it is hopeless to try to see, from where we stand now, exactly what *m/f* was: for she is still here, part of the place from which we ask the question.

As with the changed evaluation on the part of some who initially rejected *m/f*, this complicates the question that would ask what the journal's effect *was*, *then*, as definitively in the past, having happened once and for all. And for the very reason that s/he has become part of us, to see her again, now, might for such admiring readers produce a quite different impression from the one that is remembered as that of the first, formative view. If *m/f* has been fully incorporated into our ways of thinking, so that s/he is no longer separate as the new addition, out there, that we remember, it is likely that if she turned up once more, s/he would not live up to the memory of her youthful beauty, might even seem slightly aged or *passé*: to see a *passante* again might entail some unpleasant surprises that would detract from the image of her as perfect. And in this case the position is even more complicated. If the *passante* turns out to have lost some of the freshness for which we remember her, it is not because she has aged, but because she has not changed one iota or one wrinkle. Yet this is also what makes her seem out of date for us who have changed, moved on – and changed partly through the mark that *m/f* herself made on us then.

And so, reading *m/f* again, now more than ten years after the first issue, some things seem oddly distant. Parts of *m/f* return as though with a lag in their step: was *this* the one who looked so bright and promised so much? It seems to have something to do with the style. Rereading the early editorials, there is an impression of firm control, a sort of pedagogical decidedness that seems to brook no opposition or even reply,[13] and to reduce each sentence to the barest, most minimal bones of a discourse sternly connoted as plain. This raises questions, I think, about the rhetoric of feminist argument, which were not *m/f*'s concern at the time, and which perhaps show up in this way only now, when the first moment of the journal is past, and when some of the particular debates conducted or mentioned in its pages are no longer current. In these early statements of position, it is as if something in the nature of feminist argument was assumed to rule out the possibility of textual play or 'give': it is all solemnly declarative and strictly circumscribed. This is all the more striking, hard-hitting, in that the absence of play in the writing goes hand in hand, or at least side by side, with the advocacy of theories that refuse ideas of language as a straightforward, transparent medium of theoretical or political argument, as simply expressing one unequivocal thing. It is as though the exhilarating opening up of new questions in place of old protocols could only be achieved through a definitive form of declaration that partially shut them up again.

This might be connected to the intransigent styles of other left journals at the time, in whose context or terms *m/f* had to claim its right to a place and a hearing. Instead, or in addition, it might have to do with the very inadmissibility of *m/f*'s questions, whose lack of fit with feminist orthodoxies led to a form of statement that had to be all the stronger to get its point across. This raises the further question of the extent to which forms of writing or argument inflect the style of their response: *m/f*'s rejection of dogmas sometimes took quite a dogmatic form. This in turn probably had something to do with the 'all or nothing' quality of the reactions for and against the journal at the time.

P.S.

m/f thus resists not only the obviousness of sexual division, but also the simple chronology of sequential time. There is no easy temporal distinction between its appearances as young or old, new or dated; by the same token, the journal cannot straightforwardly be either forgotten, dead and buried as 'past history' or brought to new life as though it had never had any previous existence. In one way, as we have found, its re-emergence now, the *passante* returning, brings into focus as many further questions as did its first appearance. It is the first reader who is now more likely to be disappointed, and the later ones for whom *m/f* can appear, once again, in all its originality.

If the journal's effects still, in both senses, 'remain to be seen', then that is itself a sign of the challenge that *m/f* made and makes to existing ways of looking. Coupled with the use of psychoanalysis, *m/f*'s anti-essentialist crusade undermined many of the then-accepted bases of feminism. That this was taken as a threat, as well as a promise, is suggested by the force of the criticism directed against the journal. *m/f* never declared its project to be one of proposing final answers, assumptions about which were part of what it identified as problematic in the contemporary women's movement. That it was and is a source of new questions and new discussions is suggested by the appearance of the anthology, and the ambivalent legacy is in keeping with *m/f*'s enigmatic name and open questions. In one sense it left feminism without a leg to stand on, not even one, by pointing out the ways in which its apparent unity, a 'whole' body of women, was not as complete and perfect as it might look.[14] But this was also its great achievement, opening up feminist engagements and *enjambements* that might not always involve the search for single (or even double) explanatory models. Not yet that, *pas encore – m/f* was not the last to be seen or heard of the question of woman, but the questioning of woman after *m/f*'s passing can no longer be what it was.

NOTES

1 Parveen Adams and Elizabeth Cowie (eds), *The Woman in Question: m/f* (Cambridge: MIT Press, an *October* book, 1990).

2 Other partial mythological or epic echoes and sightings may then be suggested. In Book 11 of *The Odyssey*, the first of the souls Odysseus encounters is that of his mother who, in her death, gives him hope to go on by telling him news from home. Three times he stretches out to embrace her, and 'three times she flitted from my hands, like a shadow or like a dream' (22. 206–8). The episode is echoed in *The Aeneid*, first in Book 2 when the hero is vindicated in his departure from Troy by the ghost of his wife Creusa: 'Three times I tried to cast my arms around her neck where she had been; but three times, embraced in vain, the image fled my hands, like gentle winds or like a fleeting dream' (22.792–5). And later when, like Odysseus, Aeneas is granted a descent into the underworld, one of the shades he sees is that of Dido, whose presence in this place means that she did indeed kill herself when he left her. She appears out of the shadows, says nothing in answer to his questions, and 'flees back hostile into the shadowy grove' (Book 6, 22. 472f.). A widow and a queen, this woman, like Creusa, is the one who must have been abandoned for history to happen as destined, as Aeneas pursues his mission of founding Rome. There must be no regrets, and her passing appearance, dead, puts her out of the way once and for all.

3 Jacques Lacan, *Le Séminaire, livre XX: Encore* (Paris: Seuil, 1973), p. 36.

4 Ibid., p. 13.

5 Ibid., p. 69, trans. Jacqueline Rose, in Jacques Lacan and the école freudienne, *Feminine Sexuality*, eds. Juliet Mitchell and Jacqueline Rose (New York: Norton, 1982), p. 146.

6 Ibid., p. 90.

7 Lacan, *Le Séminaire, livre XI: Les quatre concepts fondamentaux de la psychanalyse* (Paris: Seuil, 1973), p. 33. This volume is translated by Alan Sheridan as *The Four Fundamental Concepts of Psychoanalysis* (London: Hogarth Press, 1977).

8 Ibid., p. 44.

9 Ibid., p. 27.

10 *m/f* 3 (1979), p. 48.

11 *m/f* 4 (1980), p. 4.

12 *m/f* 11/12 (1986), p. 3.

13 A 'worst case' example might be this extract from the first

editorial, describing one of three current 'tendencies within Marxist feminism':

> Firstly, there is the attempt to argue that women as a consistently deprived social group constitute an economic class. And because of a certain position within Marxism which asserts that transformation will be effected when a class becomes conscious of itself as a class (a class for itself) this position assumes that political changes in the position of women will be effected when women become conscious of themselves as a class. The consciousness of belonging to an oppressed class is seen to be the basis of political action. Against this argument it can simply be stated that class divisions cut across 'women as a social group'.

Three substantial explanatory sentences and then suddenly that's it – finished, dealt with (the paragraph ends there and the next goes on to a 'second tendency'). The speediness of the dismissal seems to permit no further response: it is almost a reprimand, and the quailing reader is really put in no position to think she might reasonably pay attention to this line. This is even more noticeable because it is not clear that the point is established at all. The refutation is made 'simply' by returning to the straight Marxist position that it is only the classical class contradictions that count, which is where Marxist feminist questions began in the first place.

14 If the problem of putting the psychic alongside the social was both *m/f*'s stumbling block and its most fruitful contribution to feminist debate, it might be worth glancing back at the fleeting appearance of a different kind of *passante* within its pages, one whose identity is not constrained by the impossible choice between an eternal, mythological fantasy of woman and a historically specific construction. The editorial of the fourth issue mentions an article by Parveen Adams and Beverley Brown, but there is something funny about the reference. In the third issue, where it appeared, the article is entitled 'The Feminine Body and Feminist Politics'. Now it has slipped into something a little less predictable: 'The Feminist Body and Feminist Politics'. And what a slip! Has *m/f* suddenly blown its cover, let the bag out of the bag, revealing the truth by lifting up the petticoat of anti-essentialism for just a second? Perhaps this is the first and last time that anyone, reader or spectator, ever got a glimpse of this barely imaginable entity, the feminist body. For it has never been seen again, and though no-one, feminist, woman or man, can remember what it looked like, it has assuredly left an indelible mark on the mind of every discerning reader. Love at first sight – who can doubt that the feminist body would have provided the answers to all our questions, had she but stayed awhile?

Chapter 4

'The problem with no name'
Rereading Friedan's The Feminine Mystique

> On an April morning in 1959, I heard a mother of four, having coffee with four other mothers in a suburban development fifteen miles from New York, say in a tone of quiet desperation,'the problem'. And the others knew, without words, that she was not talking about a problem with her husband, or her children, or her home. Suddenly they realized they all shared the same problem, the problem that has no name.[1]

With its specificity of time and place and its moment of collective realisation of the existence of an unnameable something, this little scene could be taken straight out of the opening of a thriller. The fact that it belongs to an argument for feminism, and that a possible word for the mysterious 'problem' turns out to be 'femininity', is suggestive in more than one way. The troubled relations and mutual definitions of feminism and femininity seem to be a never-ending serial, without the promised conclusion ever being delivered. In what follows, I shall attempt to unravel part of the plot, not so much with regard to the particular predicament of 1959, but in terms of the more general 'problem' of feminist argument and feminist ends which this passage, and the book from which it is taken, reveal.

Published in 1963, *The Feminine Mystique* is commonly regarded both as a feminist classic and as a book which acted as a catalyst to the western feminist movement which began in the mid- to late 1960s. In the canon of post-war feminist works it sits somewhat isolated, and somewhat incongruously, midway between *The Second Sex* and the outpouring of texts and tracts later on. But the striking gap between 1948 – the date of de Beauvoir's book – and 1963 in fact fits well with one of Friedan's principal contentions. The arguments of almost all feminist social critics, before and after Friedan, involve the presupposition or demonstration that women's freedom either never existed or existed only in the remote past. Friedan, however, argues that women had freedom and lost it. And this peculiarity is perhaps a starting point for thinking about some of the echoes and overtones of the unidentified 'problem'. I want to explore some of the twists and turns of this unexpected structure of feminist narrative, and how it is related to Friedan's conceptions of subjectivity, femininity and the American nation. In particular, I am interested in the links that are made between femininity, in Friedan's sense, and the impact of consumerism, and in how these links impinge upon the form of Friedan's argument.

The genealogy of Friedan's particular 'problem' goes something like this. Not long ago, in the time of our grandmothers, strong 'pioneer' women got together to claim their rights to citizenship and equality on a par with men. They won access to higher education and the professions and all seemed set, thanks to their incomparable efforts, for a fair and sunny future for the now fully human second sex. But unfortunately there came World War II, which brought young and old men flocking home to America with a craving for Mom and apple pie in the form of a wife and lots of children. To serve, or to reinforce, this need, the men of Madison Avenue stepped in. Lest there should be any women unwilling to comply with the scenario, advertising, magazines and the proliferation of domestic consumer goods saw to it that the 'image' of feminine fulfilment in the form of husband, babies and suburbia would be promoted to the exclusion of anything else. Other cultural forces came into play too. The evil prescriptions of a Freud who thought women's destiny was domestic and infantile entered and influenced every American mind. Higher education for women was dominated by a spurious use of sociology and anthropology to ensure girls got the message that their 'sex-role' as wives and mothers, and not their 'human' capacity to create and achieve in the working world, was the natural one. In any case, thanks to the bombardment of all these types of influence and suggestion, most of them left college halfway through to get married and reproduce. All the promise of a new generation of potentially free women, the daughters of the 'pioneers', has thus been knocked out of them, and it is now a matter of some urgency to expose the general fraud for what it is: to allow 'the problem with no name' to be spoken.

The dissatisfactions of suburbia centre, for Friedan, around an opposition between 'selfhood' and 'sex-role' – also glossed as 'humanity' and 'femininity'. The long-term planning and 'creativity' involved in a worthy career and valorised by Friedan against the 'stunted' qualities of the woman who remains in a state of little-girl conformity, confined her to her reproductive role and to fulfilment in the form of sex, by which Friedan means both reproduction and sexual pleasure. Motherhood, like that suburban wasteland, is a trap: Friedan has vivid metaphors of confinement to express this, including a chapter title in what now seems decidedly dubious taste – 'Progressive dehumanization: the comfortable concentration camp'. A frequently repeated image of the apparently happy housewife with 'a stationwagon full of children' is itself used to epitomise 'this new image which insists she is not a person but a "woman" ' (61). Whereas the Victorians' problem was the repression of sexuality, that of the present is 'a stunting or evasion of growth' (69).

The account of socially induced 'femininity' as inhibited growth and as something which necessarily detracts from the achievement of full humanity can be placed in a tradition of feminist humanism which goes back to Mary Wollstonecraft. Friedan's narrative difficulty, however, is that she believes that the battles of Wollstonecraft and her successors, the 'pioneer' feminists, were fought and won, and she tries to explain what she now identifies as a relapse into a situation just as unsatisfactory as the one from which women freed themselves before.

Several culprits, of disparate provenance, are identified; I mentioned some of them at the beginning. One is the spread of psychoanalysis, taken as having reinforced conceptions of women as naturally inferior and naturally destined for merely domestic functions. An *ad hominem* attack on Freud himself, via his letters to his fiancée, is used as the basis for a reading of his account of femininity, and especially of penis envy, as both prescriptive and misogynistic. Freud is effectively likened to a salesman, purveying a false representation of women's nature: 'The fact is that to Freud, even more than to the magazine editor on Madison Avenue today, women were a strange, inferior, less-than-human species' (100).[2]

Another set of culprits is 'the sex-directed educators', who have betrayed the high ideals of educational pioneers and who now offer courses which are intellectually unchallenging and whose explicit message, in courses with names like 'Adjustment to Marriage' and 'Education for Family Living', is that of the feminine mystique – Mothers' Studies, perhaps. Such education is in reality 'an indoctrination of opinions and values through manipulation of the students' emotions; and in this manipulative disguise, it is no longer subject to the critical thinking demanded in other academic disciplines' (161). The identification of a conspiracy here does not, however, stop with the professors themselves: they too have been deceived, and Friedan goes on to describe 'the degree to which the feminine mystique has brainwashed American educators' (169).

Even the brainwashers are brainwashed, then: the plot continues to thicken. Closer to home, we find a rather familiar target for blame: the mother. Not, in this case, the current generation of mystified, over-young mothers, but *their* mothers. The nineteenth-century struggle for women's rights was not incomplete. Friedan states clearly: 'The ones who fought that battle won more than empty paper rights. They cast off the shadow of contempt and self-contempt that had degraded women for centuries' (92). But then something went wrong, and it is this which she is at a loss to explain:

> Why, with the removal of all the legal, political, economic and educational barriers that once kept woman from being man's equal, a person in her own right, an individual free to develop her own potential, should she accept this new image which insists she is not a person but a 'woman', by definition barred from human existence and a voice in human destiny?
>
> (61)

The next generation did not follow up the victory, but returned to the same domesticated forms of femininity from which their mothers had sought to free them. 'Did women really go home again as a reaction to feminism?' Friedan asks, with no little bewilderment. 'The fact is, that to women born after 1920, feminism was dead history' (93). This is like saying that emancipated slaves go back to their masters when the battle is forgotten, so Friedan adds more. Feminism was not only dead history, or not *dead* history at all, but 'a dirty word', evoking for 'mothers still trapped' and still raising daughters, 'the fiery, man-eating feminist, the career woman – loveless, alone' (93). And this was what they passed on to *their* daughters: 'These mothers were probably the real model for the man-eating myth' (93). After 'the passionate journey their grandmothers had begun' as pioneers of feminism, the subsequent generations were left with no positive image with which to identify: 'They had truly outgrown the old image; they were finally free to be what they chose to be. But what choice were they offered?' (93).

The model of free choice brings us to the most often emphasised source of the feminine mystique: the media. Advertising, magazines and (to a lesser extent) popular novels and 'how-to' books from Spock to sausage rolls are treated as absolutely central to the propagation of the mystique. Friedan enters into the confessional mode in describing how she herself used to make her living writing articles to order on aspects of housewifery or mothering for magazines like *Good Housekeeping* or *Mademoiselle*. At this stage, significantly, it is tracked down as being primarily a male conspiracy;[3] and in the height of her crime thriller mode, Friedan devotes a whole chapter to the results of her being given permission to delve into the secrets of an advertising agency's market research files. It is with all the force of a revelation that she points out the importance of advertising and consumption to the social control or the sociological description of American women:

> Properly manipulated . . . American housewives can be given the sense of identity, purpose, creativity, the self-realization, even the sexual joy they lack – by the buying of things. I suddenly realized the significance of the boast that women wield seventy-five per cent of the purchasing power in America. I suddenly saw American women as *victims* of that ghastly gift, that power at the point of purchase. The insights he shared with me so liberally revealed many things . . .
>
> (199)

The image of femininity perpetrated by magazines is itself the first example brought forward by Friedan after her opening chapter on the barely articulated 'problem with no name'. She runs through typical articles and stories, showing how they share a common message and injunction to women, that they should seek their fulfilment in the form of marriage and homemaking. But, as with the history of the feminist movement, this present, univocal image is contrasted sharply with a previous phase in magazine publishing when political stories could be part of the contents list, when there were more women writers than now, and when the housewife's role was not the be-all and end-all of the reader's presumed horizons. This earlier 'passionate search for truth and identity' is highlighted by a short story about a girl who secretly learns to fly. This, for Friedan, represents the heights of past achievement and serves as a measure of how far things have subsequently declined: 'It is like remembering a long forgotten dream, to recapture the memory of what a career meant to women before "career woman" became a dirty word in America' (34).

Given the recurrent rhetoric of manipulation and brainwashing, it is not surprising that the marketing case, around magazines and advertising, should be so crucial for Friedan. The 1950s model of 'hidden persuaders' (the title of Vance Packard's 1957 book on the advertising industry) – of a barely discernible but thus all the more effective conspiracy – contributes to the mystery overtones of the diagnosis of the mystique and its origins. A distortion or 'blurring' of the image has occurred since the more open days of the flying story, so that false and fatuous models are being perpetrated throughout the land in every sphere of daily life. From education to therapy, to childcare, to journalism and advertising, women are being sold back down the river by the withholding of what ought to have been the fruits of their social emancipation. And crucially, whatever the relative priorities accorded to each of these agencies in perpetrating the mystique, it is the 'sell-out' metaphor of marketing which subsumes them all. The model of the marketing brainwash, of the insidious manipulation of advertising, is itself taken up as the model for a generalised social persuasion.

The harmful effects of the mystique are summed up by the

repeated reference to 'waste'. Waste is what happens when the
mystique takes over. The avoidance of waste represents the
kind of emotional parsimony and efficient use of available
human resources that fits with the paradigm of goal-setting
and deferred gratification. The 'waste' is first of female 'human'
potential that is going unused or untapped, owing to its
deflection into feminine channels falsely and misleadingly
imaged as leading to authentic fulfilment. Friedan is in no doubt
as to the relative valuation to be ascribed to domestic and other
forms of work: the former can be summed up as 'trivia' (230,
233), to be kept to a functional – waste-free – minimum; the
second is characterised by such heady pursuits as 'splitting
atoms, penetrating outer space, creating art that illuminates
human destiny, pioneering on the frontiers of society' (229).[4]

This unquestioned valorisation of high-flying, maximum-
penetration activities over their 'feminine' alternatives is worth
contrasting with its reversed form in a later feminist author
like Elaine Showalter. Writing in the late 1970s, Showalter
blames what she identifies as the theoreticist excesses of
literary criticism over the previous twenty years on a kind of
masculinist emulation by male critics of their scientific rivals in
the era of Sputnik.[5] Friedan has human playing feminine as
genuine plays trivial, artificial; Showalter makes the 'human
achievement' pole explicitly masculine and the alternative an
authentic femaleness.

Parallel to the idea of personal waste is that of national
waste. Here Friedan introduces a full-scale narrative of imminent cultural decline precipitated by the menace of the maraud-
ing 'mystique'. This argument acquires an urgency distinct
from the argument about women's individual waste. Friedan
refers not only to 'the desperate need of this nation for the
untapped reserves of women's intelligence' (357), but also to a
generalised domestication of all American people, men and
women. After the war, she says, 'the whole nation stopped
growing up' (178) and it suffers now from 'a vacuum of larger
purpose', from 'the lack of an ideology or national purpose'
(179). So now the infantile and non-goal-oriented attributes of
image-dominated women have been transferred to Americans
in general. And here, instead of women being the victims, they
are identified as the source. Friedan provides a whole gallery of
monstrous females, chiefly in the form of the over-dominant

mother who won't let her sons grow up and separate from her. An ideology of domestic 'togetherness' in marriage has made men so passive that even though their wives are at home all day with nothing better to do than get on with the chores, they still get drawn into the trivia of washing up, vacuuming and the rest in a way that their fathers did not.

There are indications in these sections of a nostalgia for a more authoritarian community and family structure, with mother and father each in his and her proper, traditional place and with the domestic sphere relegated to its rightful secondariness in relation to the public world of national achievement.[6] It is interesting to note the difference here from arguments in the seventies about the desirability or imminent emergence of 'the sensitive man' formed from a happy blend of 'feminine' and 'masculine' qualities – first, because clearly he figured a lot earlier, and secondly because at this stage in feminist argument he's represented as thoroughly feeble. It's not that Friedan wants to keep women in the home; rather, she thinks the home and its tasks should be reduced to a minimum so that both sexes can fulfil a genuinely 'human' function in the outside world.

More dramatically, Friedan sees 'frightening implications for the future of our nation in the parasitical softening that is being passed on to the new generation of children'. Specifically, she identifies 'a recent increase in the overt manifestations of male homosexuality', and comments:

> I do not think this is unrelated to the national embrace of the feminine mystique. For the feminine mystique has glorified and perpetuated the name of femininity and passive, childlike immaturity which is passed on from mother to son, as well as to daughters.
>
> (263)

A little further on, this becomes 'the homosexuality that is spreading like a murky smog over the American scene'. What is striking here is not only the imagery of infection – the murky disease and the clean, almost Jamesian 'American scene' – but its manifest link to a process of cultural feminisation. Male homosexuality as the end-point of the feminine mystique is not just artificial, a regrettable but accidental distortion of the reality it overlays: it is a sinister source of cultural contamination. This 'murky smog' is the final smut, the last 'dirty word' in the story of the mystique: that clean, feminine exterior is now found to hide a particularly nasty can of worms. Marketing and the mystique are together leading to 'bearded undisciplined beatnickery' (273) and a 'deterioration of the human character' (274).

Male homosexual activity is further identified as 'hauntingly "feminine" ' in its 'lack of lasting human satisfaction' (265). Friedan establishes a clear category of what she calls 'pseudo-sex' (265), as engaged in by bored housewives, teenagers and male homosexuals. Again, it is interesting to note parallels with recent arguments seen as a backlash to the liberalisation of sexual mores in the wake of the 1960s: here is Friedan making a case in 1963 for the return of real sex between real, whole people (of different sex) against a hypothetical backcloth of generalised promiscuity and a lowering of moral standards: 'For men, too, sex itself is taking on the unreal character of phantasy – depersonalized, dissatisfying, and finally inhuman' (263). The censure of 'the stunted world of sexual fantasy' (263) is exactly parallel to the criticism of the stunted image of the feminine mystique. At the same time, the obsession with sex – or with pseudo-sex – is regarded as the focal point for the diversion of women from their true selfhood. Like a Victorian moralist, or a 1980s Victoria Gillick, Friedan asks: 'Why is it so difficult for these youngsters to postpone present pleasure for future long-term goals?' (269).

And yet the argument about sexuality is not as straightforward as it appears. Friedan devotes some pages to the Kinsey reports on sexual behaviour from the late 1940s onwards, which in their revised form suggested a correlation between educational level and sexual fulfilment. She argues against pseudo-sex not on the grounds that it is immoral – though there is a didactic tone to the prose – but on the grounds that it isn't as good as it could be: 'Sex, for them [young girls] is not really sex at all. They have not even begun to experience a sexual response, much less "fulfilment" ' (265).

The further development of this occurs when Friedan suggests that real sexual fulfilment requires the other sort – 'human' fulfilment – as a condition of possibility and therefore, implicitly, that if you want good sex you should see to your achievement in other areas first. Quoting the findings of 'Professor Maslow', Friedan concludes: 'It seemed as if fulfilment of personal capacity in this larger world opened new vistas of sexual ecstasy' (311). Friedan has not herself shifted the terms from those of the mystique itself. While she accuses it of diverting women, and perhaps men too, from full human achievement to merely sexual preoccupations, her own argument is effectively to say: 'That is pseudo-sex. Free yourself from the mystique and you can have the real thing'. So sex remains at the centre; it is not so much displaced as the excesses of a passion that detracts from rationality, but rather reinscribed as an even more fulfilling by-product of personal growth.

This brings us to another equivocation in Friedan's text. She describes, as we have seen, the various institutions and agencies which might be identified as responsible for the propagation or infliction of the mystique, whatever their motives or interests. She does not really explain why the mystique appeals, why it sticks, given the prior history of tough feminist values developed and put into action in the past. The only reason, ultimately, is a negative one: women obeyed, or adopted, the mystique, because nothing better was on offer. Feminism was 'dead history' or even 'a dirty word', and a female member of the next generation was stuck 'for lack of an image that would help her to grow up as a woman true to herself' (67; cf. 355). Or in the passage quoted earlier: 'They had truly outgrown the old image. They were finally free to be what they chose to be. But what choice were they offered?' (93).

Always there is the same humanist appeal to a pre-existing individual self, embryonically there from the start and available for a development which can be straight and true or may, by extraneous social influence, deviate from its natural course. A girl either grows – grows up, tall and strong – or else she is warped and stunted and remains in a state of immaturity or corruption. Friedan claims on the one hand that the 'lack of an image' of what she might be caused the fall-back into the error of false femininity: without the good model, there is no way for the girl to grow. On the other hand, because she conceives of the person as there all the time, she also appeals repeatedly to a 'basic' or 'hard core of self' which is called upon to resist its own feminisation:

By choosing femininity over the painful growth to full identity, by never achieving the hard core of self that comes not from fantasy but from mastering reality, these girls are doomed to suffer ultimately that bored, diffuse feeling of purposelessness, non-existence, non-involvement with the world that can be called *anomie*, or lack of identity, or merely felt as the problem that has no name.

(172)

Here, it is the girl's own active 'choosing' of the femininity which then makes her passively 'doomed to suffer'. She begins as a fully rational subject and condemns herself to the utter passivity of 'non-existence'. There is a hesitation as to victimisation or agency in relation to which, in other cases, Friedan sometimes privileges one side and sometimes the other. To take another instance:

In the last analysis, millions of able women in this free land chose, themselves, not to use the door education could have opened for them. The choice – and the responsibility – for the race back home was finally their own.

(173)

In this example, free choice is real: in 'this free land', women are ultimately free to choose 'themselves', and responsible for the mistakes they make. Home is the prison they preferred to the open, outside world of education and opportunity. In the earlier example – 'finally free, but what choice were they offered?' – choice is seen as limited by what is offered. No image available, therefore no possible identification with a self to match up to the free, or freed, 'New Woman'.

This oscillation recurs throughout the book. There is the 'inner voice' within that is the germ of an authentic protest; at the same time, there is the clear statement that the image conforms in a sense to what women want: 'This image . . . shapes women's lives today and mirrors their dreams' (28–9). In other words, the 'image' imprints itself in such a way as to be indistinguishable from those other dreams characterised as more primary and more true to the inner, human self. Friedan is constantly caught in this contradiction, which can be smoothed over only by accepting the arbitrary distinction between true and false dreams – between those that are from within and correspond to 'human' potential, and those that are from without and are imposed by the manipulators of the 'feminine' mystique.

Much of the difficulty stems from the fact that the language for each alternative is identical, having to do with wanting (or 'yearning'), choice and fulfilment. Friedan tells the story of the first feminist movement, whose emergence was prompted by a situation of confinement to the home and to a state of infantile underdevelopment similar to the one she identifies in the present. The problem for a woman then was that 'she could never grow up to ask the simple human question, "Who am I? What do I want?" ' (74). But what is wrong now is articulated in terms which seem to correspond to this acknowledgement of wanting, to a search for identity and fulfilment: 'Women who suffer this problem, in whom this voice is stirring, have lived their whole lives in the pursuit of feminine fulfilment' (22).

This double premise – first, that there is a basic 'core of self' which ought to develop according to its nature and to resist extraneous influence, and second, that without an external image there is no possibility of achieving a full identity – accounts, I think, for a final twist in the form of Friedan's argument. For it is as if the entire book is there to lay out the missing image of human selfhood excluded by the mystique, but that this can only be done by repeating exactly those forms of persuasion from outside which are identified as the insidious techniques of the mystique which is thereby displaced and excluded in its turn. Be a whole person, achieve your human potential, and you can have even more than is presently on offer.

This is not to dismiss the book of *The Feminine Mystique* as an advertisers' con on a par with that of the feminine mystique it takes as its object. It is rather to suggest that the denunciation of 'brainwashing' and 'manipulation' in the name of a suppressed authenticity may mean that the authenticity claimed instead is rhetorically just as suspect. Friedan counters the mystique's representation of the natural woman with her own, and lays her argument open to the same critique in the name of another feminine – or human – nature. (And this, as we shall see, is precisely what happens when she revises her own argument eighteen years later.) In the second chapter she cites as an example of the spuriousness of contemporary women's magazine journalism an editor who was heard to demand: 'Can't you dream up a new crisis for women?' (32). Friedan's next chapter is entitled 'The crisis in women's identity'.

In rereading – or reading – Friedan twenty or more years on, it is relatively easy to point out aspects which now seem anachronistic, either because they refer to demands which no longer seem pertinent or because they appear unacceptably narrow or biased. In the first category – demands no longer relevant – would appear, for example, the fact that western nations are not much worried by high birthrates any more, or the fact that in a time of high unemployment it is no longer feasible to marshal an argument that women are a wasted asset for the state.

In the second category – demands that now appear prejudiced – would be placed the heterosexist assumptions, not only in the representation of male homosexuality as a cultural symptom, but also in the premise that the normal woman is heterosexual: Friedan refers, for example, to the 'perversion' of history by which nineteenth-century feminists are represented as 'man-hating, embittered, sex-starved spinsters' and proceeds to show, on the one hand, that many famous feminists 'loved, were loved, and married', and on the other that the cause was great enough to lead to a temporary abandonment of womanliness:

> Is it so hard to understand that emancipation, the right to full humanity, was important enough to generations of women, still alive or only recently dead, that some fought with their fists, and went to jail and even died for it? And for the right to human growth, some women denied their own sex, the desire to love and be loved by a man, and to bear children.
>
> (74)

Here there is, clearly, a conception of natural sexual difference operating alongside the claim for recognition of women's humanity; and that difference consists in a heterosexual, childbearing destiny which would radically separate Friedan from many of her feminist successors. Her argument is that marriage and motherhood should be kept in their secondary, 'sexual' place, not that they are to be questioned in themselves as part of what she calls the 'life-plan' for women.

Also featuring in this category of now unacceptable assumptions would be the middle-class, professional focus which is implicit throughout and which occasionally shows another negative side. It is in the following terms that Friedan denounces the distorted evidence used to build statistical proof that working mothers are bad for children's development:

> How many women realize, even now, that the babies in these publicized cases, who withered away from lack of maternal affection, were not the children of educated, middle-class mothers who left them in others' care certain hours of the day to practice a profession or write a poem, or fight a political battle – but truly abandoned children: foundlings often deserted at birth by unwed mothers and drunken fathers, children who never had a home or tender loving care.
>
> (185–6)

The asymmetry here between 'unwed' and 'drunken' is perhaps even more interesting than the vignette itself, with the two culpable parents stumbling around in their different states of post-natal incapacitation to throw out the baby 'at birth'. And interestingly, the 'home and tender loving care' which measure the extent of the foundling's deprivation figure here not as the false image of domestic happiness perpetrated by the feminine mystique, but as just what a baby deserves.

In academic circles, Friedan's humanist premises and triumphalist rhetoric of emancipation also now seem rather old-fashioned. The current emphasis on sexual difference as the starting point for questions, rather than as an ideological confusion masking women's full humanity, has the effect of relegating a perspective such as Friedan's to the status of being theoretically unsophisticated as well as historically outdated. But to fail to consider her on these grounds is to accept precisely those assumptions about concepts of progressive liberation and enlightenment, collective and individual, which the later models have put into question. The point is not to reject Friedan from some point of advanced knowledge either as simply 'of her time' – an argument for the early 1960s of no interest now – or as benightedly prejudiced – good liberal as she was, we've come a long way since then. Rather, the very twists of her argument, with all the oddity of its details and contradictions, as seen from more than two decades later, may themselves suggest a different perspective on current feminist preoccupations and assumptions and current versions of feminist history and feminism's destination.

Friedan's basic theory of historical, as of individual, development is one of evolutionary maturation – from 'primitive' to civilised cultures, via the agency of pioneers, in the feminist movement as in American history. In this scheme, the present form of femininity is but a moderate deviation, to be ironed out – if the image is not too domestic – by a final mobilisation of latent energy:

> In the light of women's long battle for emancipation, the recent sexual counterrevolution in America has been perhaps a final crisis, a strange breath-holding interval before the larva breaks out of the shell into maturity.

(363)

But elsewhere, Friedan half hints – and half despairingly – that there may be a structure more cyclical than progressive in the history of feminist argument. For instance:

> Encouraged by the mystique to evade their identity crisis, permitted to escape identity altogether in the name of sexual fulfilment, women once again are living with their feet bound in the old image of glorified femininity. And it is the same old image, despite its shiny new clothes, that trapped women for centuries and made the feminists rebel.

(94)

From femininity to feminism, to the forgetting of feminism to a return to femininity, to feminism again – and so on. Such would seem to be the sequence identified by this description, leaving no suggestion of a possible outcome of full feminist, or human, identity for women, since the story never ends.

This difficulty is highlighted by Friedan's own explicit shift of position since 1963. *The Second Stage* (1981)[7] reads uncannily like a reversal of the terms of *The Feminine Mystique*. In place of the silently suffering, affluent housewife, we are here introduced to the secretly unfulfilled female executive who has taken on wholesale the offer of success in a man's world but is now experiencing the effects of the 'denial' of what turn out to have been valid feminine feelings. Where 'femininity' was the false image in the first book, its negative effects to be cured by feminist consciousness, 'feminist rhetoric' has now become the stale and stultifying demand, to be cured by the recovery of a measure of femininity. Rather than the feminine mystique, it is 'the feminist mystique' which is 'the problem'. Two halves assuredly make a whole, and balance will only be attained by acknowledging the importance of those traditionally female nurturing qualities and 'needs' which the first stage of feminism forced them to repudiate.

The role of the false, distorting image played by femininity in the earlier book is thus taken over in *The Second Stage* by the 'stunting' excesses of a feminism 'blind' to the caring, family values it had to reject in order to make its initial point. In arguing that the time has now come to 'transcend' the polarisation of men and women, Friedan relies on the same types of double premises as in *The Feminine Mystique*. From one perspective, the new problems are generated by economic and national necessities (because of inflation and dwindling growth, women have to go out to work to balance the domestic budget; by the same token, macho masculinity *à la* John Wayne is no longer viable in post-Vietnam America). But at the same time, the solutions appeal to first principles: men are now able to put off what turn out to have been their own 'masks' of hyper-masculinity, to discover their underlying feelings; women, meanwhile, have got past the point of needing to assert themselves according to values now seen not as the 'human' norm but as excessively masculine. Feminism is now valorised as a buried potential, where previously it was regarded as a fabrication.

All this leaves open the whole question of what actually constitutes the difference between the sexes. Too much of either masculinity or femininity is bad for men and women, which suggests that they are not qualities tied to either sex: women must not get too much like men, any more than men should repress their feminine side. And yet, the whole aim of 'the transcendence of polarisation' is that, in the words of the book's final sentence, we will all be 'spelling our own names, at last, as women and men'. The goal of feminism, having passed through all its 'evolutionary' stages, then, would be to make true men and women of us, while at the same time the attainment of such identities is predicated on a fusion of masculine and feminine qualities. Transcendence might be another impasse after all.

This problem can be seen from another angle in the work of Nancy Chodorow, who in 1978 put forward an influential argument that makes women's mothering the central problem for feminism. In *The Reproduction of Mothering*, Chodorow proposes that the differentiated psychic development of men and women in patriarchial society is assured through the fact that it is women, not men, who raise children.[8] Change the social structure of parenting so that it is equally shared by both sexes, and you would change the psychic structure according to which boys grow up by taking a distance from women and from feminine qualities associated with them, and girls grow up ready to reproduce the asymmetrical structure by seeking compensation for their lack of power in the extra-familial world through becoming mothers in their turn.

The difficulty with this analysis is on the one hand that sexual difference becomes only an effect of differential social structures, and is implicitly effaced into nothing more than a symmetrical oscillation between mutually defining orientations towards autonomy or dependence (a man is what is socialised into separateness, a woman is what is too embedded in relationships). On the other hand, it is presupposed as basic to psychic identity. As Chodorow says in her 'Afterword': 'Equal parenting would not threaten anyone's primary sense of gendered self (nor do we know what this self would look like in a nonsexist society)'.[9]

This is exactly the problem. If sexual difference is defined only in terms of social roles, then a society in which roles were not allotted according to sex (which would be implied by a 'nonsexist' society) would presumably not mark out a distinction between masculine and feminine at all. But then it is not clear where the 'primary sense of gendered self' would come from, or why there would be any identity as male or female to be threatened.

This is analogous to the double bind of *The Second Stage*, where an acceptance of identification as a woman is thrown into question by the theoretical abolition of any basis for sexual differentiation. Just as *The Feminine Mystique* fails to ask whether there is a difference, so *The Second Stage* assumes it and at the same time abolishes it. The straightforward goal of independence put forward in the early book as women's means of becoming equal to men is simply replaced by a unisex goal of enough independence plus enough dependence. The possibility of attaining the well-adjusted harmony of the whole human self, however defined, is not questioned in either case. And it is this impasse which takes us back to what is still the unresolved mystery of *The Feminine Mystique*. In setting up feminism as a freedom gained and lost, Friedan makes problematic the easy conceptualisation of feminist progress, of the setting and resetting of agendas in view of the attainment of a known goal. The contradictions in her models of the self, of free choice and femininity, indicate all kinds of questions left unresolved. *The Second Stage* effectively acknowledges that the first stage went too far, and scored an own goal by positing its aim in terms of what is now seen as women's acquisition of a purely masculine identity. In drawing attention to the inevitability of such unequal and unpredictable developments in the histories of feminism and its definitions of femininity, Friedan shows how unresolved questions may themselves be the most suggestive clues to what remains 'the problem with no name'.

1986

NOTES

1 Betty Friedan, *The Feminine Mystique* (1963; rpt. New York: Dell Publishing Co., 1964), p. 15. Further quotations will be included within the text.

2 A full critique of Friedan's account is given in Juliet Mitchell, *Psychoanalysis and Feminism* (1974; rpt. Harmondsworth: Penguin, 1975).

3 This too is recounted in the detective mode:

I found a clue one morning, sitting in the office of a women's magazine editor – a woman who, older than I, remembers the days when the old image was being created, and who had watched it being displaced. The old image of the spirited career girl was largely created by writers and editors who were women, she told me. The new image of woman as housewife-mother has been largely created by writers and editors who are men.

(47)

4 It is intriguing that Friedan should end up by recapitulating one of the central imperatives of the ideology of housework: Waste not, want not.

5 Elaine Showalter, 'Towards a Feminist Poetics' (1979), in Show-

alter (ed.), *The New Feminist Criticism: Essays on Women, Literature and Theory* (1985; rpt. London: Virago, 1986), pp. 139–40.

6 See, for example, the section on the neurosis-free Massachussetts community of Polish immigrants described by the sociologist Arnold Green:

> Green wondered. Why didn't those children become neurotic, why weren't they destroyed by that brutal, irrational parental authority?
> They had none of that constant and watchful nurturing love that is urged on middle-class mothers by the child-psychologizers.
>
> (191)

It is as if Friedan needed to swing the pendulum all the way from maternal over-attention to (the relative sanity of) parental/paternal brutality.

7 Betty Friedan, *The Second Stage* (1981; rpt. London: Abacus, Sphere Books, 1983).

8 Nancy Chodorow, *The Reproduction of Mothering: Psychoanalysis and the Sociology of Gender* (Berkeley: University of California Press, 1978).

9 Ibid., p. 218.

Chapter 5

Soft sell
Marketing rhetoric in feminist criticism

To begin, a message from our sponsor:

> Many commodities are strictly women's propositions, and
> the advertiser, to secure the largest returns, should know
> the foibles of the sex and base his campaign upon that
> knowlege.[1]

Taken from an American advertising textbook of 1916, and
appealing to and for a type of sexual differentiation reinforced
and promoted by the expansion of marketing on both sides of
the Atlantic during this period, this quotation still has a
recognisable air. A vulnerable collective victim, 'the sex' with its
special 'foibles', is targeted by a quasi-militaristic masculine
offensive, 'his campaign'. In this case, the author in fact goes on
to suggest that the sex's particular foibles are the result of
occupational differences, rather than being natural; he does
not, for instance, suggest that marketing is only directed to or
against women, who are simply a particular case of an object
that might be any group. But in any case, the mutability of a
sex's foibles, and the fact that foibles are not confined to one
sex, is no obstacle, rather providing unlimited possibilities for
successful operations and conquests on the part of 'the
advertiser' whose sole concern is the maximisation of profit, 'to
secure the largest returns'. Marketing doesn't depend in principle on feminine foibles, as opposed to any others, but it has
generally done pretty well out of the kind of fruitful engagement suggested by the offering of 'strictly women's propositions'.

This type of exploitation (in the most literal sense) has long
been, in return, a ready target for feminist criticism. Some-

times consumerism has been seen as the principal source of women's oppression in the twentieth century, as a force which, by promoting a falsely feminine identity, distracts them from what would otherwise be their true identities, as humans and/ or as women. Such criticisms echo and are sometimes explicitly linked to Marxist and other accounts of a deterioration of the collective identity of working-class communities through the baleful encroachments of consumer culture. That this process has often been referred to in terms of 'feminisation' indicates the dominance of the quasi-sexual manipulation model of the opening quotation.

This is not the only line of reaction or resistance. Parallel to the operations of the rhetoric of marketing, there have in fact been two different constructions of the consumer to whom it appeals. In the first, of which the summary above is a version, the consumer is someone attacked by advertising as a power-less victim, her (or his) susceptibilities exploited in such a way that s/he is left with no effective choice. In the past this was usually a critical representation, whether from a liberal or a Marxist position, stressing the passive 'feminisation' of the consumer of whichever sex. The second construction of the consumer represents him (or her) not as a victim, but as the advertiser's double, engaged in conscious planning and decision-making. The sharpest British personification of this second figure emerged by the 1960s with the magazine *Which?*, designed for the thinking consumer of economical household goods. Instead of being seduced into unnecessary spending on worthless trinkets, this rational consumer is connoted as being a saver – of labour and time, as well as of money – and a sensibly functional person (s/he is more likely to buy a deodor-ant or a fridge than nail varnish or whisky). And despite appearances, not one but both of these models are implied in the types of response to consumerism described just now: one as the place of the consumer, who is deluded, the other as the place of the critic, who is not. For some time, then, the consumer has been a fairly hybrid being, half of it (more or less a feminine half) being that unhappy, or perhaps stupidly happy, victim of advertising's forces; and the other (more or less a masculine half) being a sober, rational sort of being who knows what he wants and makes the best possible decision based on the information available to get it. Meanwhile, although both these constructions remain in outline, they have undergone some extraordinary mutations of emphasis in the past few years.

The first, critical account has recently been given a more affirmative turn. Shopping is no longer seen as the despised symptom of patriarchal or capitalist alienation, but rather as part of a newly legitimate – politically acceptable – 'postmodern' interest in pleasure and fantasy. Those days are gone when consumerism could be comfortably identified as oppressive or regressive without more ado, and from some safely assumed position of exteriority. (This change is also criticised as being another weak acceptance of the status quo – a giving in on the part of the sex, and the other sex too, to a dominant order which has lately succeeded in pulling the wool or the lurex over a lot more critical eyes.)

In tandem with this (but probably seated on a different and more old-fashioned bike), the rational consumer has undergone a massive diversification of influence, with the great extension of the use of the term 'consumer' in everyday political language. The semantic territory of this figure has widened to the point where s/he has become synonymous with all sorts of other characters who might have been thought to have quite other concerns. In education, health, housing, water-drinking, egg-eating, voting and many other fields, we are all addressed as 'consumers' now, and the term is assumed to imply individual rights and respect that are lacking for those who are merely regarded as parents, patients, voters, omelette eaters and so on. The consumer is fast becoming the model of citizenship itself.

A telling illustration of this is to be found in some recent remarks on behalf of the National Consumer Council, arguing for consumer education as part of the new National Curriculum:

> Too many young people leave school knowing how to do algebra and geometry but with little or no knowledge of how to compare interest rates on different types of loans.
>
> They may be able to write an essay on Jane Austen – but unable to write a sensible letter of complaint.
>
> Throughout pupils' education, they should be encouraged to think of themselves as consumers, the council said.[2]

This takes up a long-established opposition between literature and other subjects as the irrelevant versus the practical or the socially useful. Austen's name probably serves better than those of many other writers regarded as great to conjure up the required image of trite gratuitousness, mere feminine society banter removed from the nitty-gritty of real-life problems. But what is interesting is that the 'useful' or 'socially relevant' side of the comparison should now be taken up not, for instance, by contemporary history or ethical questions, but by consumer rights and financial skills. The consumer the pupil is to be encouraged to think himself or herself is characterised simply by the capacity to demand for him/herself a decent service or product, epitomised in the unforgettable specification of the 'sensible letter of complaint'.

There has thus been an increasing use of and focus on languages of consumerism. Yet it is clear that the various types of the consumer imply different models of the mental processes of the person persuaded to buy, choose or want this or that. The consumer represented as the mindless credit-card junkie or the helpless victim of 'subliminal' techniques is a rather different subject from the one construed as a savvy selector of the cheapest toothpaste or the best school for his child. These languages are not necessarily compatible, involving potential clashes between the 'consuming passions' of the postmodern shopper and the reasonable rights of the citizen-consumer (though one 'postmodern' representation would imply a third possibility, whereby the consumer is not passive *or* rational, pleasure-seeking *or* calculating, but either, alternately, according to mood or context).

Advertisers have been interested in subjectivity from a consciously pragmatic point of view (to find out what will work as a persuasive tactic). Theorists of subjectivity have not been particularly interested in the techniques of advertising or in the debates within marketing's special branch, already established at the beginning of this century, 'the psychology of advertising'; nor have they turned their attention to the models of subjectivity implied by critics or advocates of consumerism. But despite this apparent separation, models of marketing and the consumer do make an unacknowledged appearance in some writing about subjectivity in general, and not least in contemporary feminism.

Much feminist writing about subjectivity of the past few years has sought to open up possibilities outside what it identifies as the political limits of psychoanalysis. Where psychoanalysis was brought in at an earlier moment to rupture the Marxist centrality of class to the exclusion of other categories, it is itself often perceived as being both monolithic and potentially unhistorical in its insistence on the primacy of sexual differentiation, and in a form which necessarily makes femininity into an impossible derivative of what is always a masculine norm. (I leave aside the details of this question, which I have represented only from the point of view of critics of psychoanalysis.)

In place of this, models of identity are put forward now that seek to be more flexible in their understanding of the ways in which identities, including sexual identities, may be formed and may undergo changes. Class, gender and race, as well as a variable range of other categories, are all seen to share, though not necessarily equally, in the formation of identities. At the same time, the identity of the subject is seen less as a forcible imposition, whereby she is constrained either passively to take on or hopelessly to struggle against something fundamentally negative, but rather as potentially desirable: enabling as much as it is constricting. Foucault is often cited as the inspiration for such a conception of a multiplicity of identifications produced through the operation of numerous heterogeneous discourses that pull individuals in particular, provisional directions. The political edge is maintained by stressing that the possibilities are restricted by the nature and number of discourses 'available' for identification; and the need for more or different ones is part of the argument. The aim is that no one discourse or its corresponding mode of identity should be granted priority: there can be many 'femininities', for instance, though some, according to political criteria that are given as a starting point, are deemed to be better than others.

There is, however, a particular discourse which often does emerge as dominant in such descriptions, and that is none other than the discourse of marketing and consumption. To take one example, from Chris Weedon's *Feminist Practice and Poststructuralist Theory*:

Discourses, located as they are in social institutions and processes are continually competing with each other for the allegiance of individual agents. . . .

Some forms of subjectivity are more readily available to the individual than others and this will depend on the social status and power of the discourse in question.

The nature of femininity and masculinity is one of the key sites of discursive struggle for the individual and we need only look at a few examples of forms of subjectivity widely on offer to realize the importance of this battle.[3]

Discourses behave here in a way that is identical to marketed products. As with companies' attempts to secure brand loyalty, they are 'competing' for 'the allegiance of individual agents'. One factor in deciding whether a discourse is picked up is its 'social status', just as a prominent marketing model of the consumer is based on her or his assumed need to be or appear to be higher up the scale, whether this is represented negatively, as a fear of falling ('keeping up with the Joneses'), or positively, as a desire to rise (upward mobility). There is a perpetual 'battle' (the military undertone of the advertising 'campaign') where what is being fought over is the capitulation or resistance of the consumer as territory to be subdued on a 'site' of struggle. By implication, discourses are not modified by the purchaser, but come ready-made to be picked up and used as they are. Some are more readily 'available' than others, more 'widely on offer'.

Does it make any difference to the argument to point to its hidden persuasions? The trouble arises not from the presence of this particular discourse – there is no a priori reason to think that it is more insidious than any other – but from the fact that it is taken as not in need of the analysis being given to other discourses and their processes of what Weedon calls 'naturalisation'. Charged as it is, the discourse of marketing has been taken up as neutral, and used as the framework within which to understand the operation of all discourses and the relations of subjects to them.

Since the languages of marketing and consumerism have been making their way into more fields of everyday life and talk than ever before, it becomes crucial to look out for them, not to take them as natural. But by the same token, marketing cannot just be regarded as a weed which could simply be rooted out of the discursive garden. For one thing, it comes in many shapes

and forms, in varying degrees of intensity and dis-
tinguishability. For another, like any other discourse, it did not
spring up independently, but developed out of a host of others –
the military campaign and the planned seduction are two – with
which it still enters into complicated relations, and from which
it cannot wholly be separated.

So there is no straightforward getting away from marketing
– we couldn't and need not stop using words like 'offer' or
'available'. But there should be no straightforward assumption
of its normality, either. In the light of the new pervasiveness of
languages of marketing and consumption, far beyond their first
fields of application in advertising and shopping, it becomes all
the more necessary to analyse the ways in which they work or
sell. Feminists (who, by the way, are now a key target group for
the marketers, interested in appealing to their particular
foibles) shouldn't simply take on trust, as read, the language of
advertising, which has never made any secret of having a
special interest in the exploitation of women, but which, and by
the same token, has always been most attractive to them too.

This is not simply a proposal that we should look carefully at
the labels before committing ourselves to something that may
turn out to be not what it seems at first. Instead, it seems to me
that the question of whether or not you 'buy' an argument is
already part of the problem, suggesting that an argument is
something comparable to a finished product, to be taken or
rejected as is, according to whether it seems to satisfy our
demand. The purchase of an interesting text extends beyond
the first rapid glance.

All this too might indicate that there are more general
questions to be asked about the rhetorics of feminist criticism:
about the ways in which it does or doesn't 'sell' what it is
presenting as its version of feminism; about how it sets that
apart from other versions of feminism or femininity to be
rejected; about the mode of address to the readers, which varies
from the academically authoritative to the cosily 'women
together'. Sometimes, as we saw with Friedan, feminism has
made its appeal precisely in the name of an alternative to a false
femininity identified as imposed by consumerism. For the first
issue of a feminist journal[4] whose name is not so different from
that of a mass-market magazine which used to be considered

the epitome of housewifely feminine conformity, these questions seem irresistible.

1989

NOTES

1 Henry Foster Adams, *Advertising and its Mental Laws* (New York: Macmillan, 1916), p. 317.
2 Ngaio Crequer, 'Pupils "need lessons to be consumers" ', *The Independent*, 8 August 1989.
3 Chris Weedon, *Feminist Practice and Poststructuralist Theory* (Oxford: Basil Blackwell, 1987), pp. 97, 98.
4 In April 1990, of *Women: A Cultural Review*.

Chapter 6

Flight reservations
The Anglo-American/French divide in feminist criticism

Readers of some recent works of feminist theory might be forgiven for feeling jet-lagged. The eye seems to be always overtaking some reference to the rapid theoretical crossovers and stopovers between the continents of Europe and North America, or (what perhaps comes down to the same thing) between two blocks called 'French' and 'Anglo-American' modes of analysis. Naomi Schor, for instance, in *Breaking the Chain*, wryly evokes 'the trans-Atlantic shuttle Franco-American scholars are perpetually engaged in'.[1] In a more literal flight, Jane Gallop's *Reading Lacan* recounts the respective flights of Stuart Schneiderman from Buffalo and herself from Chicago to Paris to encounter the real Lacan.[2] Alice Jardine, at the start of her book on *Gynesis*, refers to the double origin of her work:

> The structure of the questions addressed is almost wholly shaped by recent French theory. But, at the same time, the questions themselves are those of an American feminist hoping to contribute to American feminist theory. . . . But of course, even an intervention, a gesture, runs certain risks, for in attempting this trans-position, I am neither 'above it all' nor somewhere in the middle of the Atlantic.[3]

But clearly feminist theory is flying, if not as Kate Millett – let alone Erica Jong – might have wished.[4] Having taken off from the traditional grounds of fixed identities, cultural or sexual, it is playing for what seem to be markedly higher stakes.

The last two examples also suggest an element of quest-romance in the transatlantic genre. Rather than passively weave at home awaiting her man or her muse, the modern

American Penelope takes the shuttle herself to distant lands. She visits the source, and returns (perhaps to Ithaca . . .) better armed and equipped, to spread the word among her compatriots: 'Most of this book', states Jardine, 'was written in France to be read in the United States'.[5]

The problem of negotiating a cross-cultural position has indeed become a standard trope in contemporary feminist theory. And on the analogy of feminist interdisciplinary studies which aim to challenge and transform the frontiers of established schools of thought, the enterprise of questioning and working through the implications of different cultural approaches to feminism seems immediately attractive.

At the start of *Reading Lacan*, Jane Gallop devotes some pages to the question of what constitutes interdisciplinarity. She shows how this cannot be thought of simply in terms of a comparison between distinct entities – psychoanalysis and literature, or France and America, for instance. And in the case of writing a book about Lacan for an American audience, this complex framework is written into the topic from the first. Lacan's writings are shot through with a negative representation of American ego-based psychoanalysis which figures as a fall guy to make way for the counter-assertion of his own theories. So, as Gallop says in her chapter on 'The American other':

> The problem of translating or transferring the *Écrits* into the American scene is not simply to get the *Écrits* into America, but what to do about the America that is already in the *Écrits*.[6]

The anti-American tilt of much French theory cannot easily be conjured away by critics attempting to maintain a base in both places at once. It is itself part of what constitutes French theory as an alternative to what is identified as inadequate in Anglo-American thought. And this is one reason why, as I shall try to show, the differentiation of French and Anglo-American approaches tends, despite the declared project of cross-fertilising exchange, to become relatively fixed as between two separate and unequal bodies. It seems that the proper refusal of an Olympian 'trans-position' tends all too readily to fall back into the preference for one place over the other.

It has only been in the last few years that translations of *écriture féminine* have been available in English, and only a small, though now much increasing, selection. During this time, the expository introduction presenting the foreign plant in all its exotic difference has become almost a genre in its own right, always kitted out with the regulation footnote on the multiple connotations of *jouissance*. The *Yale French Studies* 1981 issue on *French Texts/American Contexts* and the Barnard conference proceedings published as *The Future of Difference* established what Domna C. Stanton called the 'The Franco-American Dis-Connection' as an ongoing question, and one which continues to structure the terms of theoretical debates.[7]

Toril Moi's *Sexual/Textual Politics* does not belong autobiographically to the transatlantic mode, since the author is a Norwegian who was working at the time of writing in Britain.[8] But it is organised around the same type of contrast between American and French modes of feminist literary criticism, through long sections dealing with each. The book is a model of lucid exposition and argument, and it rapidly and deservedly established itself as an indispensable text for both students and teachers of literary theory.

Running through Moi's readings of different critical texts is a double criterion of political efficacy and distance from conventional liberal humanism, and it is in theoretical terms identified as French that American critics are found wanting: they tend to be confined to traditional conceptions of literature as the immediate transcription of experience, and of the transcription of female experience as the mark of genuine women's literature. Such an approach, as she argues, cannot accommodate a theory of representation. It takes 'man' and 'woman' as naturally given rather than symbolic catergories, and in viewing language as a transparent medium, it reduces and refuses the complexity of the literary text. And so the book's title indicates its departure in a 'textual' direction away from what must now be seen as the too literalising argument of Kate Millett's diatribe against male authors in *Sexual Politics*: necessary as a first bash in 1969, but lacking in the analytically more complex tools that feminist criticsm has subsequently acquired.[9]

As the proportion of interrogative sentences would suggest on its own, Alice Jardine's *Gynesis: Configurations of Woman and Modernity* is a less expository text than Toril Moi's. Jardine sets out to question both the apparent ease with which Franco-American feminist differences are articulated, and the facility with which the term 'feminist' is transported between the two countries, given its different connotations in each one. The book's neologistic title invokes what Jardine perceives as a constantly recurring focus of postmodernist enquiry in fiction and philosophy. 'Gynesis' would be:

> The putting into discourse of 'woman' as that *process* diagnosed in France as intrinsic to the condition of modernity; indeed, the valorization of the feminine, woman, and her obligatory, that is, historical connotations, as somehow intrinsic to new and necessary models of thinking, writing, speaking.[10]

Or again:

> *Gynesis*: a new kind of writing on the woman's body, a map of new spaces yet to be explored, with 'woman' supplying the only directions, the only images, upon which Postmodern Man feels he can rely.[11]

'Gynesis' in this sense of an exploration of textual spaces 'gendered feminine' is located or 'diagnosed' in male writers ranging from Derrida, Lacan and Deleuze to Lyotard, Baudrillard, Goux and Sollers, all of whose theoretical or fictional undoings of 'the paternal metaphor' underpinning western discourse turn out to revolve around and explore the question of femininity.

Like Toril Moi, Alice Jardine is interested in modernist or postmodernist writing, and she links its emergence to the 'crisis in legitimation' more or less evident in western society since the beginning of the twentieth century. The loss of phallogocentric guarantees is precisely the moment at which the feminine becomes an open question: not a straightforward alternative to masculinity, or a known identity, but a virtual point towards or around which new kinds of question will cluster.

Gynesis has little to say about the issue of women's adequate representation in literature: this would be the falsely universalising, realistic criterion rejected also by Moi. But Jardine's text does frequently refer to the problematic relation between this fluid 'gynesis' located in modern writing and a female personage variously invoked as 'the feminine reader' or 'the woman reader', to whom are attributed sceptical, common-sense responses to the theoretical propositions of 'gynesis'. In effect, it is as if this 'feminist reader' is none other than the pragmatic American whose simple formulations have to be corrected and complicated by French sophistication, just as in the earlier quotation Jardine declared that her 'questions themselves' were American, but their 'structure' was French.[12] Despite the alleged interactions and mutual transformations, 'gynesis' and 'feminism' remain as distinct and opposed in Jardine's text as the French or American modes to which they are related.

The final chapter compares French and American postmodernist fiction by men, as represented in particular texts by Philippe Sollers, Thomas Pynchon and John Hawkes. While both the French writer and the Americans are concerned with the questions of interpretation, textuality and femininity, the differences, for Jardine, are crucial. Concluding the analysis of the American writers, she states:

> This is a thematization of gynesis very different from the conceptual, textual, constitutive process of gynesis inherent to modernity as diagnosed in France. The 'woman-in-effect' in American male fiction, throughout its thematization of gynesis, is as far from the most radical tenets of modernity as it is close to the conceptual foundations of, among other things, (Anglo-)American feminist thought itself.[13]

The polarisation here between 'thematization' and 'gynesis' as 'process' reproduces what it accuses in the text, and comes precariously close to the type of static binary opposition – such as 'form versus content' – from which postmodernist and feminist thought, in the different and connected ways which Jardine's book so well describes, is said to have moved on.

Even in Jardine's own account, the opposition sometimes looks forced or arbitrary. The following paragraph says why the French fictional mode is better:

> The 'she' haunting much of the most important contemporary writing by men in France is at times angelic, at times monstrous. But 'she' is always seen, above all, as that which must be explored through an erotic merging at the interior of language, through a radical dismemberment of the textual body, a female body. Woman, as identity, may eventually

reappear within the boundaries of that exploration, but never for long, usually separated from it, and always with duplicity.[14]

The 'she' as angel/monster, as ghostlike ('haunting') as dismembered body, and as duplicitous sounds uncannily familiar from somewhere. Without more specification of the difference, this could equally be read as the usual list of accusation levelled against a misogynist text, and thus as proof not of Sollers' difference, but of the fact that he remains locked in the conventional masculine fantasies of femininity which are attributed to the American writers.

It would seem, then, that however strong the assertion to the contrary, there is a tendency for the differences between American and French critical modes to be fixed into simple, homologous oppositions between stasis and process, theme and text, pragmatism and theory, realism and (post)modernism. This effect is reinforced by the representation of American feminist aims as outmoded or displaced by the passing of the universalising, egalitarian politics identified with pre-twentieth-century ideals. The universalising logic according to which women claim their rights as political subjects equal to men must now, apparently, be seen as part of a bygone stage of feminist debate; but it is also assumed to be the position from which Jardine's 'feminist reader' would put her questions to the French theoretical texts that come her way.

The dice, then, are stacked against America from the word go, as a comparison with another text further suggests. Jardine is herself one of the translators of Julia Kristeva's essay 'Women's Time', to which she refers in *Gynesis*.[15] In this essay, Kristeva identifies early feminist claims with this preliminary 'logic of homologation', or making the same, associated with republican values. She marks the end of this stage at about the date of the Wall Street Crash: an American end to western civilisation and to the patriarchal certainties which had held sway through the period of capitalism's linear, cumulative history. Like her follower Jardine, Kristeva sees the principal impact of this breakdown as the release of 'feminine' potentials and processes formerly precluded or held back by what henceforth appeared as having been a history of masculine order and repression. Though Kristeva is not convinced that 'the paternal function' can or will cease to be the lynchpin of social formations and symbolic thought, she argues that the end of logocentric linearity must imply new possibilities for the emergence or discovery of whatever the colonised 'dark continent' of femininity might prove to have been.

From this perspective, egalitarian claims, which are blind to sexual difference, can only appear inadequate or at best preliminary. The universalistic foundations on which they rest seem irreducibly tainted with the imperialism of the western nations whose supremacy is now taken to be a force of the past. Kristeva effectively identifies the end of western progress and linear time with that of the European nation, and there is a translator's footnote drawing attention to this. But in Jardine's transposition of the question in her own book, the place of the defunct European nation-state is taken by the still-surviving, goal-orientated United States. The first and implicitly subordinate stage in Kristeva's history is occupied in Jardine's by an America still present and anachronistically protesting its traditional concepts of equality and subjectivity in a postmodern era: an America whose postmodern texts, even, are not the real thing because they remain stuck in the old-fashioned grooves of logocentric thematics.

Through this brief account of one aspect of Moi's and Jardine's books, I have tried to show that there is a marked cluster or accumulation of counterposed characteristics in the use by some feminist theorists of France and America as cultural references. All the bad qualities associated with 'the west' get attributed to the United States; and where non-western cultures figure as other in relation to the west, so Europe, and especially France, can come, bizarrely perhaps, to stand in as the new or different departure from old and oppressive America. As linear is to monumental time (in Kristeva's adaptation of Nietzsche), so America is to France, man to woman, realism to (post)modernism, and so on.

This over-schematic list recalls a much-quoted passage (cited by both Jardine and Moi) from Hélène Cixous's Sorties, where she cites a series of binary pairs. One of each – as with culture/nature or sun/moon – is associated with man, the other with woman, and all turn out to be hierarchichally structured, as with what Cixous calls 'the couple man/woman'.[16] But the point of the passage, as of its quotation, is to demonstrate the reductive and subtly insidious form of just such dualistic structures. The encounter between Anglo-American and French thought is set up in the same way as a battle which has a foregone conclusion, because one side is eminently superior to the other. The slide towards a stereotypical representation signals that this framework for the articulation of feminist issues may now have become too settled, repeated and regularised as it is in a form not so dissimilar to that same hierarchical, binary fixity rightly criticised when it issues from the position of western, or American, logocentric masculinity.

There is no question of making an appeal (in the most 'Anglo-American' empirical terms) to the literal truth or falsity of particular representations of French thought on the one hand and Anglo-American on the other. The point is rather that the opposition may now have become too much of a received idea: in Jardine's terms, too much of a static 'thematization', rather than a way of putting new questions. Among other problems, it does not allow for the way in which 'French' questions have made their way in America or that 'American' issues of political rights and demands form part of the feminist debate in France.[17]

It is not impossible, moreover, that the very notion of a relatively homogeneous 'French' style of thought is itself an American fantasy, or an Anglo-American fantasy. This then raises a further question, namely the definition of the 'Anglo-American' as opposed to the French. It seems to be based on an analogy with philosophical distinctions: in Britain, 'Anglo-Saxon' or 'Anglo-American' is generally opposed to a confidently collectivised 'Continental' tradition. (And here, the designation of 'Anglo-American' philosophy started off as a generalisation on the part of the French, and so nicely suggests an inverted origin for the American, or British, fantasy of the 'French'.) But in the opposition as used in feminist theory, the distinction takes on a more overtly regional connotation – as indicated by the literal flights between France and the States – which then suggests a kind of elision of the different 'Anglo-' aspect of the phrase.

From this point it would be an easy move to offer Britain as a happy resolution or third possibility to get past the French/American impasse. It might be argued, for instance, that one strand of British feminism – exemplified in particular by the journal *m/f* – succeeded in combining 'French' theoretical with 'American' political issues, through an alliance of psychoanlysis and socialist feminism which cuts across or transcends the other pairs of alternatives. But this, once again, would be no answer. Apart from the fact that in a typically British way I am more tempted by boats or planes to France or North America, there is the consideration that putting the 'Anglo' back into 'Anglo-American' would only reinforce the literal mapping of cultural onto geographical differences. More seriously, the proposal of such a third moment to break the circulation between the two terms would fall into a traditional (and arguably masculine) dialectical paradigm. And this is precisely what is at issue in the questioning of the notion of a single or recognisable 'destination' for feminism, in the form of an American – or Anglo-American – version of 'France' or 'French theory'.

So where do we go from here? Speaking at the Southampton University conference on Sexual Difference in 1985, Elaine Showalter told the story of how she came to introduce an unplanned source when she first put forward her word 'gynocritics', which has since become established as part of the vocabulary of feminist criticsm. The occasion was a lecture at Oxford in 1978:

> As I came closer and closer to the word 'gynocritics' in my text, I became more and more apprehensive, until I had an inspiration. The word, I explained, was a translation from the French, '*la gynocritique*'. Of course, there *is* no such word in French. . . . [18]

This recounting of a pseudo-authentication may itself, of course, have been spoken tongue, or *la langue*, in cheek; but it makes a beautiful myth for the (non-)origins if the French-American difference in feminist theory. American-style feminist criticism, of which Showalter's 'gynocritics' has become an exemplary instance, is born of a fake translation out of French – as if the acceptability of a quintessentially 'Anglo-American' form of criticism for a British audience was itself bolstered from the beginning by the scholarly credentials, if not the cultural cachet, of France. Far from being incompatible, the French legitimates; and American criticism of the least 'French' variety in subsequent descriptions gives itself an impeccably continental allure.

Jardine's own neologism 'gynesis' is partly invented as a French-American differing from all too all-American 'gynocritics'. Not only does Showalter's anecdote disturb the simplicity of such a move – and not least by its deployment of the playful techniques usually supposed to be anathema to the seriousness associated with American feminism – but the word itself, with its -*esis* ending, is clearly not French (or English) in form, but Greek. 'Gynesis' thus takes 'French' and 'American' criticism back in time and away geographically from what Jardine ironically dubs the 'Parisian atmosphere'[19] in which it was written.

Is this the ultimate unravelling of the veiled text of feminity? Jardine's Greek etymology recalls Freud's analogy between the pre-Oedipal phase so significant for the girl's development and the discovery of the Minoan–Mycenaean civilisation beneath and before that of classical Greece.[20] In the exploration of hitherto unrecognised 'feminine' processes, America looks to France as France, perhaps, to Ancient Greece, or Paris to Helen – a woman who surfaces, as it happens, within Jardine's narrative:

> When we read of those who would assert that in order to have a body, one must be female; or, more pecisely, 'It is impossible to dissociate the question of art, style and truth from the question of the woman' – shall we welcome voices announcing a new historicity or must we be careful that, like Helen, we are not left in Egypt with only an image of ourselves transported to Troy as a pretext for war?[21]

The real Helen transferred from Sparta to Egypt takes the quest to Africa and borders on Freud's other famous metaphor for femininity. The 'dark continent',[22] itself much exploited in *écriture féminine*, suggests at one level the way that discussions of Franco-American differences leave out of sight other differences, on the part of non-western feminists, including many who live in France and the United States. It also points to the structure of infinite regress implied by the ever-dispersing passage away from an enlightened, over-rationalistic America in quest of a feminine something or somewhere always (un)identified as what that civilisation cannot see. And might this not be to perpetuate the endless search for truth in the form of a woman – or 'the feminine' – a search which, far from being a postmodernist invention, is as old as classical western thought itself? The identification – or deconstruction – of this quest as such is part of the aim of Jardine's book; but the transatlantic trip betwen France and America has perhaps now been repeated too often, and only leaves the judgement of woman in the gift of an idealised and beautiful Paris. Possibly, in crossing the ocean between two places whose identities are known and evaluated from the moment of take-off, the transatlantic feminist misses the chance of finding something else – a lost continent, for example – beneath the waters of the Atlantic glimpsed from the plane.

1986

NOTES

An early version of this paper was delivered at McGill University in Montreal, and I would like to thank those who were there for a helpful discussion.

1 Naomi Schor, *Breaking the Chain: Women, Theory and French Realist Fiction* (New York: Columbia University Press, 1985), p. 184. 'Female paranoia: the case for feminist psychoanalytic criticism', the chapter from which the quotation is taken, was first published in *Yale French Studies*, no. 62 (1981), *Feminist Readings: French Texts/ American Contexts*.

2 Jane Gallop, *Reading Lacan* (Ithaca: Cornell University Press, 1985), pp. 33–35. Stuart Schneiderman, a Lacanian analyst, is the author of *Jacques Lacan: The Death of an Intellectual Hero* (Cambridge, Mass.: Harvard University Press, 1983).

3 Alice A. Jardine, *Gynesis: Configurations of Woman and Modernity* (Ithaca: Cornell University Press, 1985), p.18.

4 The allusions here are to Kate Millett's autobiographical *Flying* (1974), an account of the period following the transatlantic success of *Sexual Politics*, and to Erica Jong's *Fear of Flying* (1973)

5 Jardine, op. cit., p.13. Another transatlantically complex Ithaca connection occurs via Mary Jacobus, who teaches at Cornell. In the Preface to *Reading Woman: Essays in Feminist Criticism* (London: Methuen, 1986), she states:

> To position myself as a feminist critic, both geographically and intellectually, it seems worth saying that in 1980 I moved from England to the United States. One effect of that move, paradoxically, was to take me closer to France. Recent Anglo-American feminist criticism has been invigorated, often transformed, by its encounter with French feminism, particularly psychoanalytic feminism.

[. . .] The position I've chosen to take, though often responding to the pioneering writing in the 1970's of feminist literary critics, 'herstorians', and interpreters such as Elaine Showalter, Sandra Gilbert, and Susan Gubar, seems (to me at least) to be an argument with and against the finally untheorized, experiential, and literary-herstorical tendency of much feminist criticism in the United States. (ix, xii)

Whereas Gallop raises the problem of the negative representation of America in French theoretical texts, Jacobus implicitly addresses that of the differentiation of American criticism into (good) French (an America 'closer to France', the France in America) and (less good) indigenous 'pioneering' American, a step behind.

6 Gallop, op. cit., p. 57.
7 See *Yale French Studies*, no. 62 (n. 1 above), and *The Future of Difference*, ed. Hester Eisenstein and Alice Jardine (Boston: G.K. Hall, 1980), which includes Domna Stanton's article. The publication of *New French Feminisms*, ed. Elaine Marks and Isabelle de Courtivron (Amherst: University of Massachussetts Press, 1980), was crucial in making available a collection of theoretical and political writings by French feminists to English-speaking readers. Articles or extracts from books were also published in journals such as *Signs* and *m/f*. Now, full-length translations of the work of Cixous, Luce Irigaray, Sarah Kofman, Kristeva and others are rapidly adding to the list.
8 Toril Moi, *Sexual/Textual Politics: Feminist Literary Theory* (London: Methuen, 'New Accents', 1985).
9 Ibid., pp. 24–31.
10 Jardine, op. cit., p. 250
11 Ibid., p. 52.
12 Ibid., p. 18.
13 Ibid., p. 257.
14 Ibid., p. 246.
15 Julia Kristeva, 'Women's time', trans. Alice Jardine and Harry Blake, *Signs* vol. 7, no. 1 (Fall 1981), 13–35; Julia Kristeva, *The Kristeva Reader*, ed. Toril Moi (Oxford: Basil Blackwell, 1986).
16 See Jardine, op. cit., p. 72, and Moi, *Sexual/Textual Politics*, pp. 104–5. *Sorties* forms part of the dialogue between Cixous and Catherine Clément published as *La Jeune née* (Paris: Union Générale d'Éditions, 10/18, 1975), trans. Betsy Wing with an introduction by Sandra M. Gilbert as *The Newly Born Woman* (Minneapolis: University of Minnesota Press, 1986). The quotation, which opens Cixous's contribution, is on pp. 115–16 of the French text, p. 63 of the translation.
17 For a full account of theoretical and political aspects of French feminisms, see Claire Duchen, *Feminism in France: From May '68 to Mitterrand* (London: Routledge & Kegan Paul, 1986).
     More fruitful, perhaps, than the transatlantic flight, is the direction taken by a critic like Gayatri Spivak, who has made the

interrogation both of cultural investments on the critic's part and of covertly universalising moves on the part of French and Anglo-American feminism alike a central part of her own interventions. Spivak writes as an Indian introducing French theory into the American institutional context, without any unqualified endorsement of any of these three 'positions', none of which she would see as straightforward in themselves. She questions both theoretical and political universalisations of a condition or category of 'women' (while also questioning implicitly the simplicity of that division of the theoretical and the political which has come to figure as another cul-de-sac or impasse of feminist debate).

In her contribution to the *Yale French Studies* issue, for example, Spivak points out the blind spots implicit in Kristeva's reading (in *About Chinese Women*, 1973; trans. Anita Barrows, London: Marion Boyars, 1977) of Chinese concepts of the feminine, constructed by her at the time as a possible alternative to the phallogocentric and universalising tradition of western thought. This opposition is just as reductive as, for instance, that of French and Anglo-American since, as Spivak makes clear, its implicit generalisation precludes the recognition of what distinguishes Chinese from Indian cultural forms. Spivak's anecdote about two aged Indian washerwomen she saw as a child, who still believed a piece of land to belong to the long superseded East India Company, introduces further levels of complexity: the differences between Indian women as well as between Indian and Chinese women; the relation of a colonial history to feminist theory and to cultural differences; the place, as with Kristeva in Huxian Square, of the western or upper-class feminist writing about the oppression of other women. (See Gayatri Chakravorty Spivak, 'French feminism in an international frame', *Yale French Studies*, no. 62 (1981), 154–84, reprinted in *In Other Worlds: Essays in Cultural Politics* (New York: Methuen, 1987), pp. 134–53.)

18 Elaine Showalter, 'Shooting the rapids: feminist criticism in the mainstream', *Oxford Literary Review*, vol. 8 (1986), special issue on Sexual Difference, 218. The Oxford lecture, 'Towards a feminist poetics' was published first in Mary Jacobus (ed.), *Women Writing and Writing about Women* (London: Croom Helm, 1979), pp. 22–41, and then in Elaine Showalter, (ed)., *The New Feminist Criticism: Essays on Women, Literature and Theory* (1985; London, Virago, 1986), pp. 125–43.

The remark about *la gynocritique* is certainly to be found in both places (pp. 25 and 128 respectively), and for what it's worth, I can verify as a witness at the original time and place of utterance that Showalter did indeed say this in Oxford in 1978.

19 Jardine, op. cit., p. 17

20 See Freud, 'Female Sexuality' (1931), Pelican Freud Library vol. 7, p. 372.

21 Jardine, op. cit., p. 40, quoting Derrida.

22 See Freud, *The Question of Lay Analysis* (1926), Pelican Freud Library, vol. 15, p. 313. This note is naturally dedicated to Jane Gallop,

whose *Reading Lacan* has a note confessing her inability to find the source of this much-quoted Freudian dictum, to which I owe many happy weeks in the summer of 1986 spent perusing the Standard Edition and passing on the enigma to psychoanalytically minded friends.

Chapter 7

The judgement of Paris (and the choice of Kristeva)
French theory and feminism this side of the Channel

I will begin by telling an old story about Paris. Paris, the son of Priam, King of Troy, was called upon to award the prize for a remarkable contest. A golden apple had been offered by the goddess Eris (strife). It was inscribed with the single word *kallistę*, 'for the most beautiful'. Three other goddesses – Hera, Aphrodite, and Athena – all claimed it as theirs. Paris was chosen to choose between them, as the most beautiful of mortal men (it is not said who selected him for this title or why this was the qualification for judging the goddesses' beauty). Hera offered him greatness, Athena offered him military success, Aphrodite offered him the loveliest woman for his own, if he chose them. Whether or not these promises influenced his choice we do not know. At any rate, he opted for Aphrodite and also took her bribe, since she then helped him to run off with Helen, the most beautiful mortal woman. Thus began the Trojan War, and the rest is prehistory.

This is an old story, but it seems to me that it has been repeating itself recently: behind many variations of places and roles and names, of cities or countries and individuals, the principal features of the judgement of Paris can be clearly discerned. I propose to look at one or two of them, not always pretty sights, with a partial eye to British choices and feminist concerns.

Most of the permutations involve a change to the objective genitive: the judgement of Paris becomes not Paris making the choice, but Paris as the object of choice or rejection. In the first variant, Paris, France is identified with something that is imagined as a unified, single entity of 'French theory'. There is an interested, even an impassioned gaze in the French direction, and a judgement of what the French might have to offer. What is it we see in them? What do we want of the French? What do the French make us think that we lack, or with what spectre of theoretical infection do they haunt us? For the attraction has various outcomes, as we shall see, and is accompanied from the beginning by equally impassioned manifestations of repulsion. Paris is in the place of Aphrodite, and of Hera and Athena too.

Breaking down the story into its component parts, we might say that in a first moment, we fell for it as a fairly homogeneous body, with all the French thinkers being perceived as engaged in more or less the same structuralist and/or deconstructive endeavour. It was seen as a bright new thing that would revitalise exhausted analyses, shaking up all those boring Anglo-Saxon assumptions (which probably acquired much of their stereotypical absurdity through Anglo-Saxon self-castigatory repudiations of them by identification with the saving grace of French sophistication). This was the time when ISAs were being bought and sold on every street corner, if you knew the right people,[1] and a new, hybridly hubristic translationese, crowingly defended on this side of its always already under erasure scare-quotes, was precisely signifying the break.

But then comes the second move, which starts as a fairly tentative 'I know, but all the same' – I know that French theory puts all these things in question, but all the same (even though that may be valid), it's not much use for politics – and ends with a more categorical version of this: quite simply and quite definitely, They Go Too Far. After all the heady deconstructions of teleological programmes and projects, after all the investigations, if not celebrations, of the non-unified nature of subjectivity, that old familiar friend, the 'agenda', is dusted off and put back on the table, from which the butt-filled ashtrays will shortly be emptied ready for the meeting. The party is over, and those people we met on the ferry who turned out to be not our sort after all have thankfully gone home without breaking too many glasses. Logically, it's time to put the kettle on and decide that we never liked them much in the first place, and also they were wrong, and even if they're right it's not what we need. We have grappled with the challenge of the outsider, and emerged fortified by the sense of renewed vitality, a newly defended political identity. So now Paris has been expelled for not living up to the British standards that it had also been used to put in question. That, schematically, is one version of the main strand of the story. There are more: and each, of course, has a bearing on the others, has a part in determining the different forms of negotiation, of identification and rejection. The two stages do not stand in any simple chronological relation: they overlap from the beginning, each bearing upon the righteous force of the other, and do not form a straightforward sequence of assimilation and then rejection. From whichever side, 'French theory' has appeared for the past ten or fifteen years as something that demands a reaction: as promising or threatening, as the bearer of hopes and the object of curses, to be taken on board or thrown over, preferably a good way out from Newhaven. Much of its reception has taken the form of articles ultimately condemning it, but none the less treating it seriously as the enemy to be defeated, or the means to sharpening up or perhaps modifying a previously held position.

So far, what I have said would apply generally to British left intellectual responses to French theory. But it is the vicissitudes of the feminist reception which are going to be our main interest here, and we will look at that story in more detail. As with the more general scenario, some elements of what later, in some presentations, came to be homogenised as 'Anglo-American' feminism[2] saw in theory a vital and transformative new potential. It seemed to provide sharply rigorous support for the feminist slogan 'the personal is political', but also to offer a framework in which feminism appeared not just as a liberation movement on a par with others, but as the only one which might challenge the entire order of western thinking. A new version of psychoanalysis yoked to a semiotic understanding of systems of meaning placed the concept of women at a crucial faultline, underlying the whole edifice, but also constantly threatening to break it apart. The new theories offered an account of the inescapably divided nature of subjectivity and of systems of meaning imagined as unified, and also gave good reason to suppose that women would be likely to suffer or show the effects of this differently and with more difficulty for themselves. From this it would be one short step to identifying femininity with everything that challenged or subverted the unity of meanings, projects, subjects, literature, society – and, correlatively, to identifying all these subversive elements as in some way feminine. But this kind of analysis was also seen as a problem: as diverting attention from the oppression of actual women, as far too general and removed from the specificities of social problems. Feminism too found in French theory both the catalyst, the missing ingredient that would complete it, and a potential contamination that risked destroying it.

So far, the story resembles the general outline sketched just now. But there is a further, distinctive stage in the history of the feminist reception, which was the discovery, alongside that of 'French theory' in general, of what came to be called 'French feminism'. To Anglo-American eyes, this was just as theoretical as its brother, but took a stand that was critical of or supplementary to the male writers associated with theory proper, theory all too proper. One landmark to mention here would be the publication in 1980 of the American anthology *New French Feminisms*,[3] containing short extracts from a great many different French women's writing from recent years. (The peak output of feminist writing in France itself was during a brief period from 1974 to 1976, years which produced an extraordinary profusion of publications, many still being translated now to acquire a new life in English-speaking countries.)

But the term 'French feminism' quickly became associated with three names in particular: Hélène Cixous, Luce Irigaray, and Julia Kristeva. These now were the three goddesses, chosen or rejected all together, as a homogeneous group. Articles were written in the early 1980s presenting this newfound being, the French feminist, in all her fascinating difference, for the enlightenment of the British or American feminist reader. Most often, the narrative of such articles finally offered no happy ending. First, French feminism, which the reader might think odd, would be explained, with due appreciation of the complexity of French theory for the uninitiated. Then, French feminism would be unequivocally rejected (the move of 'they go too far'), using a free choice of the standard sudden-death right-on epithets: ahistorical, biologistic, leaves out the social, all text, all sex, elitist, apolitical . . . I may have forgotten a few. A favourite word here is *recuperation:* they seem to offer all these possibilities, all this opening up of new worlds, but finally , in the last analysis, it is all 'recuperated', fails to live up to its radical potential – which is the moment at which the essay returns to its former terms of analysis, judging what it has just identified as different by the criteria that it has just said no longer apply. French feminism is admired for its revolutionary subversion of all former feminist political assumptions, then accused of not being revolutionary enough on the grounds which have supposedly been displaced.

One might be tempted to call this sort of treatment flirting with French feminism – were it not that a kind of flirtatiousness is part of what is taken to be unsatisfactory in the textual behaviour of French feminism. Too playful, too superficial, pandering to the male masters, always on about that interminable *jouissance*, as well as missing the point about larger, broader, more serious feminist agendas which, after all, we shouldn't forget in all this rush of enthusiasm for new theories. Not flirting, then, in the essays presenting French feminism, but a kind of tentative, wary handling of what always looks like quite a tantalising, rare apple, but must ultimately be recognised as being just a bit too exotic for a healthy everyday diet. Perhaps even dangerous if you don't resist the first bite, bearer of a contamination which will sap native resources all the more insidiously for seeming first to have promised to make a contribution to them.

There have been some further subplots and subsequent plots. One of these has been the move which consists of showing that this is really not the whole story of French feminism, that if we look at the 'larger picture' we will see that in France too, there are (or at least were) many other versions of feminism, many of them more recognisable in our own political terms. Another move has been that of drawing finer distinctions between the protagonists involved. Here I will highlight two particular scenarios, which both involve new enactments of the judgement of Paris, and both award the highest honours to Kristeva.

In the first, Cixous, Irigaray, and Kristeva are presented as the three goddesses between whom the choice must be made. On one side, Cixous is knocked out for subscribing to a notion of *écriture féminine* which finally sweeps away all analytical power in a vague celebration of anarchic fluidity and endless writing. Her emphasis on writing the body and on feminine *jouissance* is taken as being a problem in itself, but in any case she seems to lose sight of anything that would be specific to women by stressing the femininity, in this sense, of all great *male* writers. On the other side, Irigaray's analyses of the phallogocentrism of western thought, from Plato to Freud and beyond, and her counter-mythology of a differently structured femininity, are taken to produce no more than a straightforward inversion of the usual variations ascribed to masculinity and femininity. The femininity which subverts what is identified as the masculinity of logical coherence, projecting, or speculation turns out to look not a little like the erratic, irrational, distracted being, closer to the body and further from the social, with which women have traditionally been identified. The word is on the tip of our tongues, if not our two lips: Irigaray is out on the grounds of *essentialism*.

That leaves Kristeva maternally holding the fort (and the da) in the middle of a neither/nor schema in which she alone fails to tumble off into one or other error. Kristeva is seen to offer all the advantages of a sophisticated, psychoanalytically informed theory of the condition of femininity and of the inescapable division of subjectivity, while never falling off her horse into the adjacent pits of 'unbridled', free-flowing *écriture féminine*, or else of a too strictly side-saddled restoration of a secure and immutable notion of femininity.

There is also a second triadic scenario, in which Kristeva is pitted against two male adversaries, both of whom have had a lot to say about femininity, and both of whom have been uncomfortably taken up or else rejected in Anglo-American feminist appropriations of French theory. In this second contest, Kristeva is faced on the one hand by Lacan and on the other by Derrida. Both men are considered to have lost something along the way: Derrida a concept of the psychic, irretrievable amid a generalised textuality, and Lacan any scope for a change in the phallic economy of subjectivity – of which, on the most generous feminist reading, he at least provides a devastating analysis. Once again, Kristeva crosses the last fence here, supplying both the exploration of subjectivity taken as crucial for feminism, and the constant questioning of what it means, has meant, or might mean for women today in a world which she habitually identifies as undergoing a 'crisis' of subjectivity: this cannot be accused of being some timelessly textual or phallic universe.

The way that Kristeva's work is situated at the top of a pyramid, as the best of a choice of three, in presentations of her work and of French feminist theory generally, may recall something about a schema she uses herself in one of her most frequently read essays, 'Women's time'.[4] There, Kristeva contrasts two 'generations' of feminism which cannot be strictly separated in chronological terms, though they do have some relation to particular symbolic dates – 1929 (the Wall Street Crash) and 1968. The first generation demands equality, the right to be treated the same, to identify with the social power from which women have been legally excluded. Sexual difference is not at issue, only the righting of what should be recognised as an unjust discrimination. The second generation refuses such assimilation, identifying the social order as inherently masculine and setting up instead or alongside a 'countersociety' in the name of the feminine nature hitherto denied expression. The last part of the essay projects or imagines a hypothetical 'third generation' – beyond sexual difference in the classical binary sense, and involving an acceptance and understanding on the part of each person of the violence and division which Kristeva sees as fundamental to human subjectivity, but which the previous generations had either projected elsewhere, or taken to unlivable extremes, or not acknowledged at all, to their own loss.

What interests me for the purposes of this discussion is not so much the detail of the argument of 'Women's time', its psychical and historical terms of reference, but this recurrence of the tripartite division, with its implied dialectical teleology of a final choice established in the overriding of the other two (at one point Kristeva wryly characterises her description as 'undoubtedly too Hegelian'[5]). It is something which seems to get played out even more patently in what I have identified as further modifications of the judgement of Paris with which we began, when the arguments come to be tied to the names of particular writers.

In this connection, it is interesting that Kristeva herself selects one of these two sets that include herself when she is describing for a French readership the status of French intellectuals in the United States. In November 1988, the newspaper Libération carried an article by Kristeva entitled 'Could American culture be French?'[6] This article is interesting

for many reasons, because it is an account of the positive
'judgement of Paris' transference written from the inside. Its
implied reader is someone who is not aware of how big Parisian
intellectuals are in America. The argument is not, however,
that this importation of French thought is to be mocked as
misdirected adulation, or just a fashion. In the first section, it is
suggested as possibly being something that the 'dispersal' of
postwar American culture really does need – to give it the
coherence it lacks, to bind its fragmentation (there is a pun in
'panser leur incohérence', to bandage – and also, hearing penser, to
think – their incoherence). At the same time, there is a naive
American reception of French thinking and we can all share the
joke, knowingly needing no names named as Kristeva launches
into the judgement scene, where the three Parisian intellectuals
are to be sized up on their adopted home territory of Paris-in-
America. 'The misunderstandings multiply', she declares:

> One French philosopher becomes a new guru because they
> think they are rediscovering in him the ease of their already
> old formalist criticism ('New Criticism') to get round the
> dilemmas of history ('You're still talking about "history"?
> "the mother"? "psychoanalysis"? – these notions have
> already been deconstructed!' objects a young ingénue). A
> famous French psychoanalyst becomes a master thinker . . .
> in literature departments, though he hardly influences
> analytical practice at all. My semiological researches (the
> now famous (!) distinction between semiotic and symbolic)
> are taken as combat weapons of feminist criticism, although
> in my terms these distinctions belong to the speech of both
> sexes . . .
>
> [Ellipsis in original]

Reading this produces a sort of 'Does She Mean Us?' effect. Of
course she doesn't, she means the Americans; but that elision of
Britain in the habitual oppostition between French and Anglo-
American versions of feminism is another of the twists in the
tale that will need more thinking about.

The article continues, however, in a different vein. The next
point takes it all back with a 'however, and with all that, the
American universities are becoming the real forum where
French intellectual life, crushed by the poverty of our own
universities and the joky tone of the Paris media, is being

pursued'. Kristeva goes on to describe the 'relative autonomy' of American universities, and by the same token 'an isolation to which may be attributed their negligible influence on cultural life'. But within the universities themselves, she wonders about the effects of 'our teaching so warmly welcomed' when there seems to be a clear shift of student opinion to the right. 'Depoliticisation' is affecting Europe as much as America, but there more than here, 'the passion for politics is giving way to the taste for personal success. To do one's best, learn as much as possible, explore to the maximum: that is the objective'. There follows immediately a precise expansion of this claim:

> Women excel in this competition, and one is struck by the intellectual quality of young American women: feminism, still alive on the other side of the Atlantic, considers the recognition and intellectual success of young American women as a *political* victory.

This is a confusing sentence. The decline of politics and its replacement by an orientation towards personal success is illustrated by the achievements of women, regarded as just the opposite, a political victory, by (American) feminism. This feminism has got its political criteria wrong, but at the same time, feminism of any kind is apparently dead on the more political side of the Atlantic.

The next sentence changes tack again, this time approving an American difference, and by criteria that are by implication universal:

> However, to deplore the concentration or isolation of intellectual life in the universities alone is perhaps a reaction of another time, a democratic fantasy. By what right might we suggest the 'mass' diffusion of the intellectual sophistications descended from the sky of Hegel, Marx, Freud or Saussure, stopping over in Paris and transplanted to Ohio? Modesty perhaps requires that we go back to valuing the limited and by the same token essential role of élites. Culture is not 'massive', its requirement of distinction distances it from the media, and the civilisation of the marketplace has never been, and never will be the equal of concentrated meditation [*la méditation condensée*], even when the latter pretends it is. From this point of view, American democracy is more lucid

than we are: it creates in its universities the optimal conditions for cultivating the largest possible elite.

There are all kinds of issues which this frankly elitist paragraph might lead us to discuss, particularly us who are not so lavishly endowed with the means of university financing. For one thing, those 'optimal conditions for cultivating the largest possible elite' are cast in the logic of performativity – 'optimal conditions' and maximisation of production – which is at the same time what the 'concentrated meditation' is supposed to be defined against. For another, even if we granted the model of elitism and the relegation of the outdated 'democratic fantasy' of universal higher education, there would be numerous unresolved questions about where the boundary should come between the elite and its outside, between universities or serious culture and the market-place or the media. The most hopeful reading of the feminism example would suggest in any case that a strict boundary, a logic of mutual exclusion, would not be appropriate: otherwise success would be incompatible with true meditation, whereas a striking 'intellectual quality' is in fact unequivocally attributed to the high achievers. But this then raises more problems from the other end, if the elitism model is taken as efficient: in selecting out the best, all the best and only the best, as fit for the best education.

The main argument of the article is that the French ought to sit up and realise the admiration with which their culture is regarded across the Atlantic; but also, with 1992 on the horizon, that Paris could become the centre of a truly European culture 'from the Urals to the Atlantic', exporting itself across the ocean:

> Often it is enough to look at the French village from the perspective of the global village to notice both its limits and its promises. Could Paris be the axis of this synthesis, this cultural ferment? This is what is expected, more or less consciously, on the other side of the Atlantic, on the basis of the immense prestige which French culture enjoys over there.

Again, we cannot help wondering on this side of the Channel: 'What About Us?'[7] – closer to America than to other European countries in our traditional and regular importing of 'continental' thought , but not open to the same diagnosis as the United States of being a culture in search of an old tradition (and willing and able to pay for it).

All this may seem to be taking us rather far from feminist concerns, which in any case are evidently rather far from contemporary France – Kristeva's note to tell the reader that feminism is still alive out there, presumably in funny places like Ohio. But let us return briefly to a passage in an interview Kristeva gave back in 1974, published with the title 'La femme, ce n'est jamais ça', 'Woman is never that', 'Women can never be defined', which may have some relevance here:

> To think one 'is a woman' is almost as absurd and obscur-antist as to think one 'is a man'. I say almost because there are still things to obtain for women: freedom of abortion and contraception, crèches for children, recognition of their labour, etc. So 'we are women' still has to be maintained as an advertisement or slogan for making demands [comme publicité ou slogan de revendication]. But, more profoundly, a woman, that cannot be: it is even what doesn't fit into being [ce qui ne va pas dans l'être: also, 'what is not right with being']. Given that, a woman's practice can only be negative, going against what exists, to say that 'it is not that' and 'it's not yet'.[8]

This has always struck me both as extremely suggestive and as harbouring a lot more questions, and it seems so even more in the context of the article from which I have just quoted, with its pat distinction between meditation and the media. For what can it mean to imply that political demands are to be seen as a form of advertising? The contrast is implicitly between on the one hand a public, collective sphere using the techniques and the language of commercial media, and on the other a constant questioning, perhaps something like that 'concentrated medi-tation' of Kristeva's more recent piece. Yet then, as before, there is immediately the problem of where to place the bound-ary between the two, or how to establish which questions fall into which category. (Is it clear, for example, that reproductive rights would be automatically something to be advocated as an advance for women from Kristeva's psychoanalytical point of view? Wouldn't they be just the sort of area where there might be much more to be thought out? In relation to issues like that of surrogate motherhood, the slogan 'the right to control one's own body', which rests on the model of an autonomous subject with the power and the right to make fully rational decisions, comes to seem even less self-evident in its implications than it already might be in the case of abortion rights.) This is not to denounce slogans, but rather the assumption of a neat separation between slogans and thought (or politics and theory, perhaps), and the covert condescension to the obviousness of slogan-led politics (no more to say). For it also seems to me now that part of the attractiveness of Kristeva's formulation here, providing both a politics and the scope for a continual questioning, itself derives from its memorable simplicity. It is itself a kind of slogan, but one that does not rule out the possibility of its being further interrogated, a questioning and questionable slogan.

So I do not want to finish by producing yet another scene of the judgement of Paris, by choosing or rejecting a new goddess or a familiar one. My point is not that we should triumphantly knock *The Kristeva Reader* off the mantelpiece because we have purloined a letter not intended for us in which Kristeva reveals what she really thinks about the American star system, and her faith in a global elitism based on American funds and French intellect. But perhaps on this side of the Channel, in a country which has neither the dollars nor the ideas in anyone's mythology (including our own), we may at least (it's a little least but it's something) be in a position to think in ways that have nothing to do with a hypothetical distinction between 'concentrated meditation' and vulgar mass media, and in which we have no need to identify ourselves as either the naive importers or the proud resistance in relation to prestigious French culture.

Perhaps up till now we have been too pious in our responses to French theory and to its individual representatives: not only in becoming wide-eyed disciples, but also where we have shown a tight-lipped refusal of interest. This would seem to lead us to partake of the worst of both Kristeva's postmodern worlds: a snobbish elitism (the chosen few, those in the know and privileged to provide the correct interpretations of the masters' texts), and media hype (the fascination with the idols).

In the case of feminism, I have tried to suggest, where arguments have not focused on the presentation of a general difference between two entities called 'French' and 'Anglo-American' feminism, they have tended to concentrate on the merits or otherwise of theorists taken as single authorial figures, to be defended or accused or explained as if they were offering, or failing to offer, universal blueprints. We have wanted them to provide us with the answer, deified them when they seemed to supply it, and blamed them for falling short of it. But we could have a differently interested response, which I see no good reason to call 'concentrated meditation' – for me that expression has a monastic ring to it that I don't readily associate with feminist thinking. Particularly now that so much more work by French women thinkers is becoming available in English, it is possible to take it up or leave it alone other than as an imagined unity (of author or cultural origin). If this is dispersal rather than concentration, it is not, as in Kristeva's representation of America, the ailment that French thought is brought in (or bought in) to bind together, but rather, perhaps, a way of making our judgements less final and our capacities for attachments, political or intellectual, more open to different forms of work and love. And if that makes any sense, it's a sense that is probably derived, most of all, from the writings of Kristeva.

NOTES

This paper was written for a day-long conference in May 1989, at the South Bank Centre, organised by Helen Carr, on 'Contemporary French Philosphy and the Revolutionary Tradition'. It formed part of the session on French feminism, at which Nicole Ward Jouve also spoke, on the *psych et po* group.

1 Louis Althusser, 'Ideology and ideological state apparatuses' (1970), trans. Ben Brewster, in *Lenin and Philosophy* (London: New Left Books, 1971).
2 See further chapter 6 in this volume.
3 Elaine Marks and Isabelle de Courtivron (eds), *New French Feminisms* (Amherst, Mass.: University of Massachusetts Press, 1980); published in Britain by Harvester.
4 Julia Kristeva, 'Women's time' (1979), trans. Alice Jardine and Harry Blake, in *Signs*, vol. no. 7, 1 (Fall 1981); reprinted in Toril Moi (ed.), *The Kristeva Reader* (Oxford: Basil Blackwell, 1986), pp. 188–213.
5 Kristeva, 'Women's time', p. 203
6 Julia Kristeva, 'La culture américaine serait-elle française?', *Libération*, 22 November 1988, p. 7.

7 Echoing Gayatri Spivak's complaint that Kristeva overlooks India in her dichotomy between Indo-European and eastern traditions in *Of Chinese Women* ('French feminism in an international frame' (1982), in *In Other Worlds* (New York: Methuen, 1987), p. 140).

8 The interview was reprinted from the journal *Tel Quel*, vol. 39 (automne 1974) in Kristeva's *Polylogue* (Paris: Seuil, 1977), pp. 517–24. It was translated (as 'Woman can never be defined') by Marilyn A. August in Marks and de Courtivron (eds), *New French Feminisms*, and also in a shortened version by Clare Pajaczkowska in *m/f*, vols 5 & 6 (1981), pp. 164–7.

Chapter 8

Still crazy after all these years
Travels in feminism and psychoanalysis

BLIND DATES

Not so long ago, I was looking around in the attic and came across some documents written in a script that was virtually indecipherable to me, and thoroughly enigmatic. I was interested and not a little perplexed by them, and devoted some time to trying to puzzle out their meaning. Eventually, I felt I had succeeded in breaking the code – though the documents came from a bygone civilization of which I knew nothing, and I may have gone off on the wrong track altogether. They seemed to feature the same two personages (if that is the proper term) again and again; but I think they were written by diverse hands, so I cannot be sure if what I thought I was putting together was a simple story, stage by stage, or whether it was the same event – if there was an event – told from different and conflicting perspectives. I will provide a few examples to show you what I mean:

ξ, highly intelligent, discontented, 29, wishing to settle down, seeks ψ

in hope of further developments . . . ψ, prepossessing in appearance, late 30s, flourishing legal practice, seeks ξ for enlightening conversation . . . ξ, still looking, seeks theory of why she is so unhappy. ψ welcome.

ξ still discontented, seeks theory of why she is so unhappy. ψ need not apply . . . ψ met his friend ψ_2 in the bar. He said to him: What the hell *do* they want? And the consequence was that they both had a good laugh at her expense. . . .

ξ met her friend ξ_2 at a conference. She said to ξ_2: I get nothing out of my ψ.

ψ is the cause of all our problems. ξ_2 said to ξ: ψ is the answer to all our problems. There were more
conferences [consequences?] . . . ψ, qualities as ever, still interested in ξ, but asks sincerely: What do you want?
ξ, not what you think, wants . . . [there may be a gap here; or there may not]

I was intrigued by these various stories and their various outcomes (and I have only given you a fraction of the material at my disposal). They seemed to offer no definite conclusion, and might have been written by many different authors. Who were these characters ξ and ψ, and were they the same in each of the little samples? Why did they keep coming back to each other after the end of the story; or why could they never seem to get it together? My material was so fragmentary and blurred that it was difficult to know how to date it – whether all the pieces came from the same period, or whether they were scattered over a very long time. Nor was it possible to know whether the 'dates' they seemed to be setting up had ever moved from possibility to reality. Was I just dealing with the coy imaginings of some cosy Victorian parlour game, or was this the record of buried events of burning and hitherto unrecognised importance? I decided, at any rate, to devote such investigative powers as I could muster to examining this mystery – a mystery which, as I was fully aware, might well turn out to lead me, to coin a phrase, up the garden path, if not on the road to wilderness. For it might turn out that the mystery was in fact nothing other than the pretence of one: the solution would be that there had been no mystery after all. Yet how could I ever establish this? If the fragments held no secret, this could never be proved conclusively, once and for all: there would always be the chance that there was a further layer to uncover, something that I could never fathom. These reflections, however, were not conducive to sanity: that way, I said to myself with firmness, madness lies (or tells the truth, perhaps). So I decided to proceed along the path I had set for myself, without looking back.

I only wish that what I am about to tell you could be presented in the form of a coherent, linear narrative, leading inexorably from its starting point to its conclusion. But what I found was that the peculiar and piecemeal quality of the raw material kept coming back, if I may say so, to 'unstructure' my own account of how I tried to discover its source. I dare say I was led off along many false tracks – how could it be otherwise, when I did not know where I was going, or even whether there was a destination at the end? Given the strange character of my material, I encountered many problems of translation, and if my solution of these language difficulties seems at times tendentious or impudent, I can only protest that I was of course speaking 'tongue' in 'cheek'. No doubt I trailed too many wild geese, was led astray by a succession of shaggy dogs, flogged not a few dead mares. I can honestly say, though, that whenever I saw a cat I took no further steps and merely called it a cat, *mewtatis mutandis*, or even (perhaps) *per os*.

But inevitably, then, I am going to tell some tall stories and some small stories – many pre-modern. If I did not find the solution to the enigma, I may at least have stumbled on some of the reasons for why it remained one. To put it another way, I think I found the key to the door, but not whether anything lay on the other side of it.[1]

TILL DEATH DO DRIVE US APART

To begin at the end, then, an excessively clear and schematic summary of the current state of play (or the permanent state of play) for the two protagonists. Psychoanalysis and feminism, it seems, have been together for a long time now, fixed into what seems to have become a virtually interminable relationship, marked repeatedly by expressions of violent feeling on both sides. Passionate declarations are followed by calm periods and then by the breaking out or resurgence of desperate denunciations and pleas once again. Past periods or episodes – Freud and the hysterics, the 'great debate' of the 1920s and 1930s – are dimly glimpsed or resuscitated, long-forgotten dates, taking on renewed if not new meanings from the perspective of contemporary interests. Vehement denials and vehement advocacy characterise the proposals of both parties. 'We were made for each other', says one partner in the first flush of rapture; only to be followed at a later, more bitter stage by a transformed insistence that 'the relationship was doomed from the start'. The one constant seems to be that neither side ever lets go: even when far apart, between their scattered blind dates – the 1890s, the 1920s and 1930s, the 1970s and 1980s – they have always somewhere been on each other's mind.

Both sides accuse the other of conforming to cultural edicts which they should rather be challenging. For the anti-psychoanalysts, an awesome 'Freudianism' represents the reimposition of the law of patriarchy by which women have always been oppressed, and so is detrimental to the cause of women's emancipation. These feminists see in psychoanalysis an endorsement, rather than a critique, of just what makes patriarchal society unbearable for women. For the pro-psychoanalytic feminists, the problem lies rather with (the rest of) feminism's assumption that the identity of women as women (and men as men, for that matter) is unproblematically given, or that difficulties of sexuality and conflicts of subjectivity are no more than the effect of contingent social oppression. Psychoanalytic feminism takes non-psychoanalytic feminism to be too simple in its notion of subjectivity for it to be capable of achieving the very political goals it sets itself; while antipsychoanalytic feminism sees in the psychoanalytic stress on subjectivity a needless detour from feminism's real concerns, if not a pernicious undermining of the tough, coherent agents needed to carry through political action with a subjectivity united at both the individual and the collective level.[2]

It is thus not only that feminisms for and against psychoanalysis have trouble in knowing how they feel about each other, but also that these difficulties come to be related to problems of how they identify each other's position. The psychoanalysis that one side sees as the cure, or at least as an account of the working of the disease, is seen by the other as just another instance of the same infection, all the more insidious for being misrecognised as its mitigation. Psychoanalytic feminism claims that feminism needs an extra edge of questioning that only psychoanalysis can supply, while non-psychoanalytic feminism argues in its turn that feminism is quite radical enough on its own and would only fall back into the very traps from which it is trying to free women by taking up with a psychoanalysis irretrievably tainted with conservative, masculine norms.

The issue, repeatedly, revolves around deciding what is to be considered truly political for feminism: one of the baselines of the argument is the implied legitimation in terms of the gesture of 'more political than thou'. And it is in relation to this that the double question of origins and ends arises: where are women's difficulties supposed to have started; and where does feminism think it is going? Is psychoanalysis a time-wasting diversion from the principal goal; or (from the other side) has the feminism that ignores psychoanalysis taken a short cut that will only return it to the same questions in the long run?

BUT WE HAVE SO MUCH IN COMMON

If psychoanalysis and feminism seem to be locked into combat or copulation unto the death – and the choice of which one depends entirely on the viewpoint of the spectator – then it may come as less of a surprise that they could be said to have been together all along. The *Oxford English Dictionary*, completed in 1933, has no entry for psychoanalysis. Feminism is listed, but with just one citation, from 1851, meaning 'the qualities of females', together with the curtly italicised information: *'rare'*. If feminism were a naturally female quality, perhaps it would never have had to be invented; at any rate, in the first *OED Supplement* – which in fact appeared in the same year as the dictionary was completed – both psychoanalysis and feminism are allotted a place, and in recognisable guises, with detailed entries both for themselves and for their loyal practitioners, the feminist and the psychoanalyst. Psychoanalysis, for which the first English usage is recorded in 1906, is supplied at the start with an author and a geographical location – it is 'a therapeutic method for treating certain disorders elaborated by Dr. S. Freud of Vienna' – and there follow some further details. Feminism is defined cumbrously and perhaps undecidedly as 'the opinions and principles of the advocates of the extended recognition of the achievements and claims of women; the advocacy of women's rights'. But the entry begins emphatically: 'Delete *rare* and add'.

In the *OED* context – English at its purest – it is significant that both words are presented as foreign imports. Psycho-analysis is said to be taken from the German as well as invented by the named Viennese doctor; feminism is attributed to the French *féminisme* (though more specific filiations lie behind that, as we shall see).[3] It is as though English, if not England, stands in need of additions which will complete it, become part of its own language and culture, but which can only be thought from abroad. And this is paralleled by the specific logic of the *Supplement*: part of the dictionary but yet an extra, an addition; something in which it has been found to be lacking, and which it cannot do without in order to complete itself, but which is none the less situated as external and separate. Psychoanalysis and feminism share the same relationship to the legitimating English dictionary as one of those advocated as the relationship linking psychoanalysis to feminism: feminism cannot do without a psychoanalysis which is yet something other than it (and the same would be true the other way around).

Not only, then, are psychoanalysis and feminism joined together until death, but also the pair apparently have in common the same moment of birth, like twins destined for endless love and rivalry from the very beginning. Sharing a kind of quasi-legitimacy, neither fully integrated nor unequivocally cast out, they both owe their official introduction to the anglophone world to the *OED Supplement*. It is as if they were both fated to be marginal to official Englishness, placed off-centre (but placed none the less) and deriving their critical force (or perhaps their ineffectiveness) from just such a doubtful position, not quite inside and yet not absolutely excluded or ignored.

TRIVIAL PURSUITS

The possibility, or inevitability, of mistaken identification – each side seeing in the other what it longs for or what it dreads – seems to be built in to the structure of this case. Perhaps there is no relationship between psychoanalysis and feminism. Or perhaps the blind dates that seemed to be suggested in the historical fragments with which we began will offer some further insights. If the couple are unknown to each other, there is first the possibility for boundless expectations in the imagining of what the other party may have to offer. Disappointment gives place to disillusionment; but then, after a period of temporary forgetting, the whole thing can start up again, with both partners blind to the fact that they have ever met before. What becomes more disturbing in this perpetual restaging of the same passionate drama, the same old serial, is that it might be quite literally a programmed repeat, with no differences at all. If every move, every question, and every answer is entirely given in advance, a perfect copy of an unchanging script, then the joke of the blind date is not only on the hapless participants, but on the spectators trying in vain to maintain their belief in the 'live' spontaneity of the proceedings – or perhaps, finally, not caring one way or the other. An allusion to Cilla Black's infamous television show, where the jokes are all pre-written and the blind dates are spectacularly predictable, may seem out of place in the serious context of the dates, or rather debates, between psychoanalysis and feminism. I bring her on stage, or onto the screen, provocatively, as the doubtful *dea ex machina* who will guide me to what I want to suggest is a serious question about triviality.[4]

Both psychoanalysis and feminism throw into confusion ordinary conceptions of what is to be considered as 'merely' trivial; and not least – though not necessarily from the same angle – in terms of what constitutes the basis for the 'obvious', everyday distinction between the sexes. Freud says towards the beginning of his 'Introductory lecture' on 'Femininity': 'When you meet someone, the first distinction you make is "male or female?" and you are accustomed to make this distinction with unhesitating certainty'.[5] This is the distinction which is so automatic, so 'unhesitating', as to go without saying; and for that very reason, as he will go on to suggest, all the more liable to question. The triviality of the example – that everyday encounter with an unknown person – reverses the implications of the 'accustomed' grid, the habit becoming suspect precisely because it is habitual.

But there is more to triviality than this. The word is derived not from a binary but from a triple distinction: the Latin 'trivium', *tris viae*, 'three ways'. In the context of psychoanalytic stories, this indicates a further step back, from Latin into Greek and Sophocles' play about Oedipus, where the event that may or may not have taken place when the hero, travelling many years before, killed an old man at the intersection of a crossroads, a 'triple way', becomes a question of the utmost importance.[6]

There is another point at which psychoanalysis comes upon a crossroads at which three ways, three roads, lead off. This is none other than the crucial original encounter with that other person as 'male or female': the mythical moment of 'fright' at first sight when the meaning of sexual difference impinges upon the child.[7] And at this juncture, each of the two trivially obvious sides of the distinction turns out to be broken down into three different possible ways. For the boy, the realisation of the girl's lack sends him off along one of three lines – homosexuality, fetishism, or 'normality' – which respond to his newfound vulnerability. Feminist priorities mean that we do not have time to follow the boy's adventures further. For the girl, there are also three possible 'lines of development' – to neurosis, to the 'masculine protest', or to 'normal' femininity – and we shall have occasion to return to them later on.[8]

BOY MEETS GIRL?

One of the difficulties in bringing about or rejecting the desirability of a final union between psychoanalysis and feminism has been precisely that of identifying the sexes of the two parties. From the point of view of anti-psychoanalytic feminism, the person of Freud as a Victorian patriarch is usually taken as the ground for assuming an inescapably anti-feminist stance built into the texts and the practice of psychoanalysis ever since. 'Dora', who walked out before the conclusion of her analysis by a Freud who had not recognised his own interest in seeing her desire as simply heterosexual, can be regarded from this point of view as the first heroine of feminist protest against a psychoanalysis which was doing no more than reconfirming the prevailing sexual norms. From the other side, that of pro-psychoanalytic feminism, Freud's early researches into hysteria mark the starting point of what was to be an undoing of every bourgeois or patriarchal assumption as to the biological naturalness of heterosexual attraction, or the masculinity and femininity predicated of men and women.

The first OED Supplement example for the word 'feminism' may possibly be enlightening here. It dates from 1895, and reads: 'Her intellectual evolution and her coquettings with the doctrines of "feminism" are traced with real humour'. This might alert the reader to a possible danger in assuming too easily a convenient equality or symmetry in the origins of psychoanalysis and feminism in Britain. Here, as the inaugurating example, the 'very first' instance which will set the terms for the established meanings of the word, we have something that appears to be just the same old misogynist bar-room joke. Not only is feminism in quotation marks, but it is something merely to flirt with – temporarily, perhaps, on the way to a womanhood that would have nothing to do with 'feminism'. The relation between the 'intellectual evolution' and the 'coquettings with "feminism" ' is not specified. They might be complementary, reinforcing each other as reason and emotion. They might both be taken as delaying the arrival at normal femininity, but only in the sense of predictable 'phases' to be treated with indulgent paternal 'humour'. Or feminism might be considered the principal deviant: all intellectually evolved women are likely to go through a feminist 'phase'. As a last possibility, the two might be antagonistic, the feminism militating against the intellectual development or the 'coquettings' distracting the brain.

The exemplary first occurence of feminism (or rather 'feminism') begins, on closer scrutiny, to look more and more like a miniature illustration of the questions surrounding the psychoanalytic account of femininity. Does this vignette postulate the implied relationship between intellect, feminism, coquetting and the acquisition of a 'normal' femininity as something that calls for explanation, or rather as a matter of course, obvious as the difference of the sexes? Is the choice of a first citation for feminism in which these moments are said to be treated with 'real humour' an exposé of the standard smutty jokes at women's expense whose structure Freud lays bare, or is it just one more example of them?[9]

Oddly or inevitably enough, 1895 is also the date of the completion of Freud's and Breuer's *Studies in Hysteria*, in which the 'cases' analysed raise all the same questions as does this questionable 'case' of feminism as to the pertinence of the psychoanalytic account of feminine development. Either the hysterical women analysed by Freud and Breuer open the way to a general understanding of the typical structures which make femininity difficult for women, or they inaugurate an ineradicable complicity of psychoanalysis with the same notions that make all women into aberrant 'cases' for masculine correction or contempt, and make feminism into a permanent joke between men.

It is perhaps quite appropriate that the English girl should be 'coquetting' with feminism, the word carrying with it all the quintessentially English connotations of its Frenchness. 'Feminism' is French too, according to the dictionary; the pair seem to be well-matched, and heterosexually, since it is with men that girls are supposed to coquette. And further investigations with the French dictionary reveal that feminism is in fact ultimately a masculine word – not only by grammatical gender, but in that Fourier is specifically named as its (male) inventor: 'Le mot "féminisme" fut créé par Fourier'.[10] This makes feminism's kinship with Dr Freud's personalised psychoanalysis take on different implications. In its origin, as in Freud's interpretation of it, it apparently represents a 'masculine' line of development. Or, like psychoanalysis, its beginnings seem to have the form of the father's kindly intervention to set the dissatisfied girl to rights. An investigation of the source of the coquetting quotation makes things no simpler; but we will not allow ourselves to be waylaid by this here.[11]

The question of the relationship between intellectual evolution and femininity is one that is broached by Freud, too, quite soon after this, for instance in a footnote to the 'Dora' case, where he refers to 'her declaration that she had been able to keep abreast with her brother up to the time of her first illness, but that after that she had fallen behind him in her studies'. He goes on:

> It was as though she had been a boy up till that moment, and had then become girlish for the first time. She had in truth been a wild creature; but after the 'asthma' she became quiet and well-behaved. That illness formed the boundary between two phases of her sexual life, of which the first was masculine in character, and the second feminine.[12]

It is also significant that at the time when Dora was presented to Freud for analysis, she 'employed herself . . . with attending lectures for women and with carrying on more or less serious studies'.[13] Read with hindsight, the passage can be seen as foreshadowing what will later become the definitive Freudian account of femininity as predicated on the giving up of what is first of all, but equally with hindsight, a masculinity shared by children of both sexes. In the meantime, the structures of castration and the Oedipus complex have been fully installed in Freud's theory, to make the 'boundary' between the 'two phases' of the girl's life acquire all the sharper a distinction.

YOUR PLACE OR MINE?

There is a famous passage at the end of one of Freud's last essays, 'Analysis terminable and interminable' (1937), which is partly about the difficulty of bringing a long relationship to an end, and which throws some more light on this difficult passage or connection between masculinity and femininity. Freud writes:

> We often have the impression that with the wish for a penis and the masculine protest we have penetrated through all the psychological strata and have reached bedrock and that thus our activities are at an end. This is probably true, since, in the psychical field, the biological field does in fact play the part of the underlying bedrock. The repudiation of femininity can be nothing else than a biological fact, a part of the great riddle of sex.[14]

This is one of those places where Freud seems most open to the charge of biological reductiveness, on the grounds – the 'bedrock', no less – that he makes of an untenable femininity, femininity as by definition to be repudiated, femininity as the point below which analysis can go no further, the bottom line which cannot itself be further broken up into component or underlying parts. The monumental impenetrability of a geological formation seems to be set irrefutably as the natural base for sexual difference.

But, as with all such pronouncements in Freud's texts, it turns out that the conclusion can be turned on its head. For Freud is using what he calls 'the biological factor' as his foundation for making a statement which in fact removes masculinity and femininity from the order of direct relationship to male and female bodies. Rather than their being natural outgrowths or symmetrical identities, the man's identity as a man is founded, as a footnote makes clear, on the fear of castration, on the denial of being a woman.

But, this departure from the biological 'bedrock' still leaves us back where Dora started – merely transposing the problem to another level or layer. The form of the asymmetry or discontinuity of masculinity and femininity remains a problem. There is no equivalent insistence for the woman that she is not a man – no repudiation of masculinity – and to the extent that there can be said to be a first, more natural identity, it is masculine, not feminine:

> In females also the striving after masculinity is ego-syntonic at a certain period, namely in the phallic phase, before the development to femininity has set in. ... A great deal depends upon whether a sufficient amount of her masculinity-complex escapes repression and exercises a permanent influence on her character.[15]

Femininity is thus the place where no man – male or female – wants to be, and its repudiation is the attitude that characterises both the 'normal' man and the woman who has remained masculine, refusing or failing to change her first, masculine nature for femininity. Even though Freud characterises the repudiation of femininity as an immutable, quasi-biological given in this essay, he does not appear to be treating it as necessarily a universal attribute of women. Instead, it would seem to apply only to the 'masculine' line of development and not to the 'normal' feminine woman whose masculinity has been adequately repressed.

Now this quotation is the best-known, but not the only Freudian occurrence of 'repudiation' in relation to femininity. In 'The psychogenesis of a case of female homosexuality' (1920), we read: 'After her disappointment, therefore [in relation to her father], this girl had entirely repudiated her wish for a child, her love of men, and the feminine role in general.'[16] This description would fit with the later essay, in that repudiation goes together with the adoption of a masculine attitude (here related to the woman's 'masculine' adoration of a woman).

But there is a further instance which complicates this relatively straightforward paradigm. In the 1933 lecture on femininity, published four years before 'Analysis terminable and interminable', in the same year as the OED Supplement, repudiation turns up in the summary of the 'three possible lines of development' that lead off for the girl following 'the discovery that she is castrated':

> Her self-love is mortified by the comparison with the boy's far superior equipment and in consequence she renounces her masturbatory satisfaction from her clitoris, repudiates her love for her mother and at the same time not

infrequently represses a good part of her sexual trends in general.[17]

Here, repudiation is explicitly linked to the two changes – in relation to the chief place of her erotic arousal, and to the sex of the one she loves – which the girl, who now turns out to have been 'masculine' up to this point, has to make in order to become a woman. The recognition of sexual difference in the form of her own lack brings with it the recognition that the formerly phallic mother is no better off, and therefore to be 'debased in value', as Freud puts it at the end of the paragraph. The repudiation of the mother, which goes along with the general depreciation and devaluation of 'the woman', by women as well as by men, is the repudiation of her as feminine.

Freud has enumerated the three possible 'lines of development' for the girl as being to sexual inhibition or neurosis; to the masculinity complex; or to normal femininity. The context does not make it clear which of them is being described at this point. Freud begins the paragraph by announcing it as referring to the line to sexual inhibition or neurosis. The line of masculine protest is subsequently given a separate exposition, but the third line, to normality, effectively blurs into the neurotic line, so that it is justifiable to see the passage above as covering both where they deal with renunciation and repudiation: it is the degree of sexual repression that distinguishes the two. And here we seem to have come upon an unexpected turn of events. In the other two examples, the repudiation of femininity was symptomatic of neither of these, but of the third line, that of the masculinity complex. Now, far from being confined to one of the three 'lines', the masculine one that ought to be furthest from normal femininity, the repudiation of femininity has come to characterise all three, including that of femininity itself.[18]

A little later in the 'Femininity' lecture, Freud refers to 'the wish for a penis being *par excellence* a feminine one'.[19] This might seem to be logical on the grounds that if anyone is going to wish for the thing, it will be the woman, who does not have it. But previously, femininity has been characterised as the end-point which implies the woman's coming to terms with the fact of her castration, rather than continuing to resent or seek to remedy it, in contrast to the still-protesting woman who is hopelessly wanting what she can never have. Freud says this explicitly in another of the *New Introductory Lectures*: 'It is also easy to follow the way in which in girls what is an entirely *unfeminine* wish to possess a penis is normally transformed into a wish for a baby'.[20] There seems to be something of a contradiction here, and stated in exaggerated form: the wish for a penis is 'entirely unfeminine', and it is *'par excellence'* feminine. A longer version of the second passage may perhaps make matters clearer, since it too is concerned with the achievement of femininity through a baby. The passage states:

> Often enough in her combined picture of 'a baby from her father' the emphasis is laid on the baby and her father is left unstressed. In this way the ancient masculine wish for the possession of a penis is still faintly visible through the femininity now achieved. But perhaps we ought rather to recognize this wish for a penis as being *par excellence* a feminine one.[21]

The second passage reinterprets the first, which insists that femininity is precisely not the wish for a penis – 'entirely unfeminine' – by emphasising instead the continuity, given that the baby-wish simply takes the place of the penis-wish: it is its substitute and it is also what hides its continuing existence. But removing a contradiction has only produced the scandal. There is no place of femininity at all: femininity itself is still 'the masculine wish for the possession of a penis'. Even the properly feminine woman is still caught up in the masculinity complex, still hankering after a penis, even if this is covered over by the wish for a baby, and still repudiating the femininity she is said to have attained. If it seemed at first that there were three roads, of which only one led to the 'final' destination of femininity, it now seems that all roads lead to the same destination, or rather to the same non-destination, the same repudiation.

A THICKER ENTANGLEMENT

In view of this loaded background in the texts of Freud, it is intriguing that 'repudiation' is a word which has often appeared or recurred in arguments over the proper relationship between psychoanalysis and feminism. To begin with the opening page of Juliet Mitchell's *Psychoanalysis and Feminism*, the book which launched the present engagement: 'It seems to me that we have turned things on their head by accepting Reich's and Laing's analyses and repudiating Freud's'.[22] Then Jane Gallop, analysing Mitchell's criticisms of those who criticise Freud on biographical grounds declares: 'Interestingly, the repudiation of the trivial *ad hominem* argument returns continually'.[23] In Jacqueline Rose's fine reply to Elizabeth Wilson's criticisms of psychoanalysis, the word occurs a few times in relation to both the British left and British feminism, in their joint or separate 'repudiation' of psychoanalysis. What Rose calls 'a fairly consistent repudiation of Freud' is also a fairly consistent application of the term 'repudiation' by those who are for psychoanalysis to those who are not.[24]

Given the cluster of associations which link repudiation and femininity in the Standard Edition, it may well be worth examining the implications of this recurrent charge in some detail. For 'repudiation', even aside from its Freudian uses, is not, after all, just any old word. It is strong language, and seems to imply not just rejection or refusal, but also that what is rejected is somehow a part of the repudiator: that it is illegitimately cast off. Repudiation's five emphatic syllables seem to proclaim their refusal a little too loudly. There is the implication that what you repudiate really belongs to you, stays behind to haunt you, however hard you try to get rid of it. Repudiation carries the suggestion of an arbitrary gesture which is not concerned with arguing in terms of moral rights or logic. In this respect, the word is precisely differentiated from its near homonymic neighbour 'refutation', which has – or had, until it began recently to be used as synonymous with 'disagree' – just that dispassionate reason which repudiation lacks. Or put the other way round, repudiation has all the emotional conviction to which refutation is indifferent.

Returning to the *OED* for more rational or impartial enlightenment, we find there are further layers to be uncovered. The primary meaning, now defunct, of the verb 'repudiate' is specific and revealing. It is 'to divorce', and it was used in English of a man in relation to a woman but not the other way around. In the expansion t1at follows the initial definition, we have first: 'Of a husband: To put away or cast off (his wife): to divorce, dismiss'; and then 'cast off, disown (a person or thing)'. If we put this piece of information back into the context of the relation between psychoanalysis and feminism, the situation seems all the more confusing. To say that feminism repudiates psychoanalysis is to put feminism in the position of a man rejecting his wife, in a gesture that could not be reciprocated. It means that the feminist rejection of psychoanalysis is equivalent to an exemplary instance of the exercise of patriarchal power; it means also that there is no position other than that of an identification with patriarchal authority from which it can be done. And if repudiation connotes the putting asunder, at the instigation of one of them, of two 'persons or things' which were to have been joined together for life, it suggests a newly literal side to what are claimed as the 'fatal' consequences that would ensue on feminism's refusal to couple itself with psychoanalysis.[25]

The use of the term 'repudiation' by advocates of psychoanalysis seems then to have the effect of a double bind – or rather, a forced marriage. It accuses feminism of acting with the arbitrary prerogatives of a representative of patriarchy, of inserting itself into precisely the paradigm from which it wants to free women, and on the side of masculine power. If feminism accuses psychoanalysis of merely validating the established forms whereby women are supposed to find their fulfilment as wives and mothers, psychoanalysis turns this back on feminism by declaring it already married to a psychoanalysis from which it can only be separated by itself re-enacting or reinstalling those structures of patriarchal authority: repudiation is just one of the lesser-known and more patriarchal of the fifty accredited ways to leave your lover.

Bearing in mind all these complexities, some old-fashioned 'feminine' sympathy is perhaps not out of place for the heroine or victim of one of the dictionary's examples of the word, taken from the *Edinburgh Review* of 1803: 'She does not appear even to have understood what they meant by repudiation'. Now this poor lady so patronisingly chided is in fact none other than Madame Suzanne Necker, the mother of Madame de Staël and the wife of Louis XVI's minister, Jacques Necker. In 1794 she published from exile in Switzerland a book on divorce. But we don't have time to pursue this lead any further . . .[26]

There are still further layers to be uncovered: we have not reached 'bedrock' yet. The English 'repudiation' is a direct import from the Latin *repudium*, which is in turn cognate with *pudor*, meaning 'shame', whence in English the (still Latin, euphemistic) *pudenda*. Literally, the *pudenda* are simply 'parts for which shame should be felt'; the use of the word (in Latin as later in English) to refer only to the female genitals is an interesting case of the figure of part for whole (or rather hole for whole). A single instance of nebulous neuter 'things for which shame is appropriate' comes to take the place of the entire class. Both the euphemistic equivocation and the generality of the *pudenda* serve as a thin veil for the word which in practice can mean only one thing. It is the female genitals, in their lack by comparison with those of the man, which figure as the ultimate cause in Freud for the disparagement of femininity, for the determination on the part of protesting men and women to be exempt from such a meagre and shameful endowment.[27]

All this leaves us with some contradictory consequences. In psychoanalytic theory, supported by linguistic fossils if not by human anatomy, there is apparently no case of repudiation which is not, at bottom, at rock-bottom, a repudiation of femininity. There is further no attitude to femininity which is not that of repudiation: thus no place, once past the crossroads where the question 'male or female?' is first posed or imposed, that does not imply the repudiation of femininity, including the place of femininity itself, which is *repudianda*, to be repudiated, for feminine women and feminists alike. And this merely repeats the fate of the *pudenda*, themselves concealed inside the word: there are no shameful parts other than the parts which are those which distinguish, or rather diminish, the woman. Repudiation implies the taking of a masculine position and the rejection of a feminine one; at the same time there is no escape from that femininity which is everyone's cast-off or ex-wife, be they man, feminist, or lady.

So where does this leave psychoanalysis and feminism? If repudiation is always the repudiation of femininity, then in its own terms psychoanalysis can hardly blame feminism for an attitude which it has identified as inevitable. This is perhaps just a different inflection of that old psychoanalytic saw about Dostoevsky's 'knife that cuts both ways', to which Freud alludes in a footnote about – what else? – feminist objections to psychoanalysis: any objection to psychoanalysis can always be intepreted psychoanalytically, as can the psychoanalytic account of femininity, which then leads to 'no decision'.[28] Psychoanalytically, it is impossible to adopt psychoanalysis (which is what the sceptics are being urged to do): it cannot be repudiated. To put it bluntly, the knife that cuts both ways is also the three ways that fork only one way. You can't refute it to which we may now add: you can only repudiate it.

All this may provide some kind of explanation for the interminability of the courtship of psychoanalysis and feminism. Psychoanalysis is certainly accusing feminism of taking a masculine stance. But even more significantly, it is putting itself in the impossible place of the woman. For just as they are locked into a state of mutual denunciation, each accusing the other of acting like a man, so they come straight back together in their joint claim that something should speak from the position of the cast-off woman.

THREE WORDS IN A BOAT

But further discoveries await us. So far we have been assuming that there is some kind of textual justification for the connection we have been making between the various Freudian feminine repudiations. But if we go back behind the familiar words of the Strachey translation to take a look at the original language of psychoanalysis, a startling revelation awaits us. For it turns out that the German word translated by 'repudiation' is different in each of the three cases noted above. In the 'Femininity' lecture, it is *verwerfen*, meaning 'to throw away' or 'discard'. In the 'Analysis' essay, 'repudiation' translates *ablehnen*: ' to decline, refuse, remove'. And in the 'Female homosexuality' text, it is *weisen*, in a construction where it means ' to exile, expel, or banish'. These words are not identical in meaning or in force.[29] In fact, the mildest word, *ablehnen*, is the one which occurs in the most intractable, most often cited passage, the one which makes the repudiation of femininity into the 'biological "bedrock" '. In view of the fact that 'the repudiation of femininity' has become one of the most familiar phrases in anglophone discussions of Freud and femininity, this assimilation on the part of the translator, deliberate or not, seems to be worth some attention. 'Repudiation' covers three different German words in the same context of an attitude to femininity; the three words are themselves used elsewhere in Freud without being translated by 'repudiation'.

Just as in Freudian theory the obviousness of 'male or female?' must be broken down to show the three ways offered to each sex at the point of that initial separation, so the 'repudiation' of femininity which has turned out to dominate, even to block, all the possible paths seems now to be itself made up of three different words, hitherto unsuspected beneath the familiar, unified cover. Arguably, then, the decision can be seen retrospectively to have marked a turning point in the future possibilities for discussions of psychoanalysis and feminism. Perhaps, indeed, it may have inaugurated a distinctively English, or anglophone, 'line of development': 'No femininity please, we're British'.

We could then carry this to the limit, and ask what it would mean if 'the repudiation of femininity' were nothing but an error of translation, a bad English dream that has been marring the fates of femininity and feminism ever since. What a momentous difference would then turn out to have ensued when psychoanalysis crossed the Channel and arrived in Britain: at one stroke, we might then have found the answer to why psychoanalysis has never made its way into British culture, or why English-speaking feminists have been reluctant to adopt it as a theory. What a relief, or a shock, after all these years, if the trouble could all be blamed on an idiosyncratic predilection, say, for that satisfying and rare five-syllable word – or else just on the slightest assimilating slip of the Strachey pen. Legend has it – and I have not been able, despite earnest researches, to find the source[30] – that when Freud arrived in the United States to deliver a series of lectures in 1909, he said of his new science and its new destination: 'We are bringing them the plague'. It would be a nice irony if the plague with which the Standard Edition infected the English-speaking world was not Freud's psychoanalysis at all.

But the problem cannot be put in such clear-cut terms – all the more so since the clearness of the cut is precisely what is at issue. Instead, the multiple origin of 'repudiation', raises more general questions about the necessary interpretation and distortion that accompany the translating and the transporting of theories from one language and culture to another. There are also the issues surrounding the gesture of a 'return' to the texts of Freud – questions which are particularly risky at this point because one of the German words translated as 'repudiation', *verwerfen*, is also the word from one of whose uses in Freud Lacan extracts the concept of foreclosure associated with psychosis.[31] It might be argued that there is a crucial difference in the two moves: Lacan is openly admitting that he is drawing out implications which are not thematised in the master text, whereas Strachey, who says nothing about what he is up to, is smuggling in his plague upon women by the back port, in the guise of a direct rendering. But the moral terms of this could just as easily be put the other way round: Strachey is the simpleton who does not realise the significance of what he is doing, while Lacan is claiming as faithfully Freudian something which is actually not there in the original. Putting the issue like this sets up dividing lines which only send the question back to the problem of the master text: to distinguish between the honest importer and the pirate, between the judicious and the blind interpretation, involves just the same appeal to the initial text as the rock which harbours the pure ore of indisputable meaning. The straight and the stray translation are indistinguishable: the 'Strachey' translation. Even if it could somehow be demonstrated that the 'repudiation of femininity' did not correspond to 'what Freud really said' or 'really meant', this would not cancel out all the arguments about psychoanalysis in English that have been carried on in the meantime: it would simply be the vehicle of a further stage in them.

Now that the rock of repudiation has been shattered, or at least its impenetrability put in question, do the three German words that lie beneath it offer us any potential way out of the impasse of femininity? One meaning of *die Verwerfung* is that of a geological fault: using the translator's licence in reverse, we could put this back into the passage from 'Analysis terminable and interminable'. In this sense, it would seem that 'the biological "bedrock" ' was not the repudiation of femininity but the faulting of femininity, leaving open, in the slide between the strata, the possibility that there might be further to go after all, a still more 'basic fault' that had previously not been seen.

The gap between German and English takes us back to the meaning of *weisen von sich*, 'to exile or banish', in the passage from the 'Female homosexuality' case. The word 'repudiation' has itself exiled, repudiated, the femininity that might not have been so utterly ruled out in the German original. This story of a forced exile is also, of course, that of the girl's sudden and shattering realisation of the significance of her sex and her doomed departure on a one-way ticket to the far land of femininity that never comes, or at which she never arrives.

And what of the time before that? For Freud uses the motif of feminine exile in an explicit and famous simile: 'Our insight into this early, pre-Oedipus, phase in girls comes to us as a surprise, like the discovery, in another field, of the Minoan-Mycenaean civilization behind the civilization of Greece'.[32] Let us pause for a moment with this Minoan-Mycenaean civilization that was producing such archaeological excitement in Freud's time, the layers of an even more ancient Greece below the one that had previously been thought to be the bedrock, the furthest back or down that there could be. It is generally dated about 1400-1100 BC, and has been the source of much evidence for the society from which the Homeric poems and the legends of Greek tragedy then turned out originally - in their first, orally transmitted, form - to derive. It had been thought that this society was non-literate; then came the discoveries of tablets with writing, and the eventual deciphering after many years of the script known as Linear B. Here are some Linear B ideograms:[33]

It is from this other Greece that Freud takes his analogy for the world of the girl before the discovery of her castration.

Imagine, then, lovely Rita, the psychoanalytic girl, her illusions ruined, forced to emigrate from the world of Mycenae into civilization, having to make that choice between three journeys that is no choice after all. The travel agent, who has seen it all before, demands the usual excessive price and explains the various options: 'It will be the trip of a lifetime'. He hands her the standard brochure. It is in twenty-four blue volumes, very heavy for travelling. She takes one look and casts it back in disgust: 'It's all English to me'. But it is too late – the ship is already pulling away and her mother is bidding her goodbye with a repressive wave from the quayside.

Now imagine, several millennia later, the psychoanalytic girl, still travelling. She has been to Phrygia, to Protest City. She has been to Vienna, to Berlin, to Paris; she has crossed the sea to London and sailed across the ocean to New York. Then she was in France again, and lately she has been attending many international gatherings. Never has she come anywhere near to the promised destination of Normal, in the state of Femininity, and in any case she has never been able to avoid the feeling that it does not sound like a place where she would like to end up. She is tired out and disappointed with the trip that cost her so much, longing for home in spite of it all; she is inclined to think that the agent ripped her off. With great difficulty, she procures a passage back to Mycenae, telling herself that she might have been mistaken in the reasons for leaving which seemed so pressing at the time.

She travels for many miles, and eventually the landscape starts to seem familiar. The old town looks the same as she steps down from the train, except that the station seems to have been modernised. There is no more grass, but there is a big tree, to which some zealous bureaucrat has pointlessly attached a label bearing the word 'tree'. And what do those signs mean on the doors over there? She never saw them (were they there?) when she was a girl, but now in a flash it hits her that they must be the same as the ones she has seen at every stop on her journey. Just in time, with a well-trained feminist instinct, she jumps back into the compartment, and away she goes again.

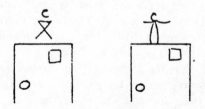

She thought she loved, she thought she was full of love. This was her idea of herself. But the strange brightness of her presence, a marvellous radiance of intrinsic vitality, was a luminousness of supreme repudiaiton, repudiation, nothing but repudiation.

Yet . . . in this state of constant unfailing repudiation, was a strain, a suffering also . . .

. . . why need she trouble, why repudiate any further. She was free of it all, she could seek a new union elsewhere.[34]

NOTES

1 For (possibly misleading) clues to these extracts, the reader is referred not to the door (which will be tried again in the course of this investigation), but to Freud's 'Dora': 'Fragment of an analysis of a case of hysteria' (1905), Pelican Freud Library (hereafter PFL), vol. 8 (Harmondsworth: Penguin 1977), p. 119. Also in *The Standard Edition of the Complete Psychological Works* (hereafter *SE*) (London: Hogarth Press and the Institute of Psychoanalysis), vol. 7, p. 82.

2 On this point see Angela Weir and Elizabeth Wilson, 'The British Women's Movement', *New Left Review* 148 (November/December 1984), pp. 74–103.

3 For another deployment of English and French dicitonary examples and definitions of feminism, see Alice Jardine, 'Men in feminism: odor di uomo or compagnons de route?', in Alice Jardine and Paul Smith (eds), *Men in Feminism* (London: Methuen, 1987), pp. 54–5.

4 For the uninitiated: Cilla Black, 1960s Liverpool pop star, has acquired a second wave of fame as the presenter of a British TV show called *Blind Date*, which is loosely modelled on the American *Dating Game*.

5 Freud, *New Introductory Lectures on Psychoanalysis* (1933), PFL, vol. 2 (Harmondsworth: Penguin, 1973), p. 146; in *SE*, vol. 22, p. 113

6 Sophocles, *Oedipus Tyrannos*, 800f.

7 'Probably no man is spared the fright of castration at the sight of a female genital', 'Fetishism' (1927); 'The little girl, frightened by the comparison with boys, grows dissatisfied with her clitoris', 'Female sexuality' (1931), PFL, vol. 7 (Harmondsworth: Penguin, 1977), pp. 354, 376; *SE*, vol. 21, pp. 154, 229.

8 Parveen Adams's 'Of Female Bondage', in Teresa Brennan (ed.), *Between Feminism and Psychoanalysis* (London: Routledge, 1989), analyses the three lines of sexual development further.

9 For Freud's analysis of the structure of the dirty joke, see *Jokes and their Relation to the Unconscious*, PFL, vol. 6 (Harmondsworth: Penguin, 1976), pp. 140–6. Also *SE*, vol. 8, pp. 97–102.

10 'The word "feminism" was created by Fourier'. The Robert dictionary is here quoting Braunschwig's *Notre littérature étudiée dans les textes*; the date of Fourier's invention is given as 1837.

11 Just a little here, though. It is an anonymous review in the *Athenaeum*, 3522 (27 April 1895, p. 533), of a novel called *The*

Grasshoppers, written by Mrs Andrew Dean. 'Mrs Andrew Dean' is a pseudonym for the much more plausibly named Mrs Alfred Sidgwick, who wrote some thirty-five novels spanning a period from the 1890s to the mid-1930s. The short *Athenaeum* account does not shed much light on the precise configuration of femininity in *The Grasshoppers*; the sentence informing us that 'the most elaborate portrait . . . is of the terrible German aunt – a vicious semi-lunatic of the most deadly kind' may tell us more about the contents of the reviewer's late-Victorian mental attic than about Mrs Sidgwick's novel itself. The titles of her other works are in fact tantalizingly suggestive in matters of feminine psychology and feminist argument: they include *Below Stairs, The Bride's Prelude, Law and Outlaw, Maid and Minx, Masquerade,* and *A Woman With a Future.* It is perhaps not purely a flight of fanciful speculation to wonder about the themes they seem to share with the writings of Mrs Alfred Sidgwick's exact authorial contemporary, Dr Sigmund Freud, especially since another of her novels was called *The Professor's Legacy.* Closer to home, and bearing in mind Mrs Sidgwick's evident achievements in her feminine, if not her 'feminist', line, we scan with some interest the much shorter list of publications by *Mr* Alfred Sidgwick. And it is rather difficult to resist the suspicion that he might have felt he had something to prove or disprove when we note, in addition to the relative smallness of their number, the fact that one of his books was entitled, firmly and laconically, *Fallacies.*

12 'Dora', PFL, vol. 8, p. 119; SE, vol 7, p.82.
13 Ibid., p. 53; p. 23.
14 'Analysis terminable and interminable' (1937), SE, vol. 23, p. 252.
15 Ibid., p. 251
16 'The psychogenesis of a case of female homosexuality' (1920), PFL, vol. 9 (Harmondsworth: Penguin 1979), p. 384; SE, vol. 18, p. 158.
17 Freud, *New Introductory Lectures*, p. 160; SE vol. 22, p. 126.
18 Ibid., p. 162; p. 129.
19 On the convergence of the three lines, see further the first chapter of Luce Irigaray, *Speculum: Of the Other Woman* (1974), trans. Gillian C. Gill (Ithaca: Cornell University Press, 1985).
20 'Anxiety and instinctual life', ibid., p. 134; italics mine.
21 'Femininity', ibid., p. 162.
22 Juliet Mitchell, *Psychoanalysis and Feminism* (1974; rpt. Harmondsworth: Penguin, 1975), p. xv.
23 Jane Gallop, *The Daughter's Seduction: Feminism and Psychoanalysis* (Ithaca: Cornell University Press, 1982). p.5.
24 Jacqueline Rose, 'Femininity and its discontents' (1983), in *Feminist Review* (ed.), *Sexuality: A Reader* (London: Virago, 1987), p. 177 *et passim.*
25 For the 'fatal' quality of this relationship, see Juliet Mitchell, *Psychoanalysis and Feminism*: 'The argument of this book is that a rejection of psychoanalysis and Freud's works is fatal for feminism' (p. xv). If this feminism here says to psychoanalysis, 'I cannot live

without you', or (to the rest of feminism), 'Without it, we will die', then just as forcefully, those on the other side proclaim that it is precisely psychoanalysis that is or would be 'fatal' to feminism. Elizabeth Wilson declares: 'In the Freudian or more fatally in the Lacanian account, the organization of difference not only does but *must* occur around the dominant symbol of the Phallus' ('Psycho-analysis: psychic law and order', in *Feminist Review* (ed.), op. cit., p. 179).

For a different exploration of the 'marriage' of psychoanalysis and feminism, see Jane Gallop's chapter in Brennan, op. cit., n. 8.

26 Or just a little perhaps: see further the *Edinburgh Review*, vol. 1 (January 1803), pp. 486–93. The article's running head, 'Mad. Necker, *Reflexions sur le Divorce*', referring to the new edition of the book in question, is indicative of the writer's attitude to the question of the intellectual development of women which was raised in relation to Dora: 'Though we are not disposed to assign any limits to female acquistions in literature or erudition, the display of them ought to be attended with some caution. . . . She may be a sort of prodigy in her own circle, without having acquisitions beyond those of a boy of sixteen' (p. 493).

27 This might also suggest some underground connections – not etymologically founded, this time – between 'repudiation' and another of its close neighbours, 'reputation'. For just as surely as a woman is subject to repudiation, so she is awkwardly situated with respect – or with disrespect – to the notion of reputation. Repu-tation's basic meaning, according to Webster's dictionary, is that of 'the state of being well reported of, credit, distinction, respectability'. But 'a woman with a reputation' is a woman without a reputation – she has lost it or she never had it in the first place. 'A woman of good repute' has to be differentially marked by the positive term: she is guilty until proved innocent, and, as with repudiation, ordinary justice does not apply. If she is to be granted a reputation for something other than sexual virtue or immorality, then it will not be a woman's reputation. In the same way that repudiation comes down to the repudiation of the woman, and repudiation of the woman comes down to that of her genitals, so a woman who gets herself a reputation is always tainted with a specifically sexual shame. And just as the initial disparagement is what pushes her from one extreme to the other, to take on the perfect reputation of the chaste goddess or guardian of morality, so 'prudery', another near homonym, is in effect the sexual shame of femininity taken too literally, to the point where it veers over into caricature.

28 Freud, 'Female sexuality', PFL, vol. 7, p. 377; *SE*, vol. 21, p. 230.

29 I thank Ulrike Meinhof for her help with the linguistic aspects of this section.

30 This note is left blank for the insertion of that source.

31 See further the entry under 'forclusion' in J. Laplanche and J.-B.

Pontalis, *Vocabulaire de la psychanalyse* (Paris: Presses Universitaires de France, 1967), pp. 163–76.

32 Freud, 'Female sexuality', PFL, vol. 7, p. 372; *SE*, vol. 21. p. 226.

33 These examples are taken from Lilian H. Jeffrey's article on 'Writing' in Alan J. B. Wace and Frank H. Stubbings (eds), *A Companion to Homer* (London: Macmillan, 1963), p. 550. They show man, woman, and olive tree.

34 D. H. Lawrence, *Women in Love* (1921), ch. 19, 'Moony'.

TRIVIAL ALLUSIONS

As well as those directly noted, quotations or near quotations from the following works (among others) have been used: Michael Balint, *The Basic Fault*; The Beatles, 'Lovely Rita'; David Bowie, 'Suffragette City'; Sigmund Freud, *Fragment of an Analysis of a Case of Hysteria* ('Dora'); Tom Jones, 'The Green, Green Grass of Home'; Jacques Lacan, 'The agency of the letter in the unconscious', and *Encore*; *No Sex Please We're British*, the title of a long-running London show; Elvis Presley (and later The Pet Shop Boys), 'Always on My Mind'; Ferdinand de Saussure, *Course in General Linguistics*; Paul Simon, 'Still Crazy After All These Years' and 'Fifty Ways to Leave Your Lover'; Oscar Wilde, 'The Sphinx without a Secret'.

Chapter 9

One foot in the grave
Freud on Jensen's Gradiva

Feminist explorations of Freud's conception of femininity always seem to run up against some bedrock or impasse which means that the hypothetical woman ends up forever out of sight. Either she is long buried in the ruins of a Minoan–Mycenaean past, unable to take any part in the modern world, or else she has got herself lost on the way by taking one of the roads marked out for the man she can never be. One way or the other, she is divided between masculine and feminine identities, unable to settle with either, since neither is simply available for her taking. Wherever we look in Freud's discussions of femininity, the same difficulty seems to emerge, as though from a rock formation so deeply embedded that it would take something like a volcanic eruption to shift it.

At one chronological end there are the writings on hysteria, culminating in the 'Dora' case, which make of a feminine illness the paradigmatic site of a trouble besetting human subjectivity in general. In their 'suffering from reminiscences', hysterics reveal an inescapable division between past and present times, between wishes and reality, between actual and forgotten objects of love; such disarticulation will form the basis of the developing psychoanalytic model of a self that is never fully settled in one place, one time, one identity. At the other chronological end, in the articles of the 1920s and early 1930s, femininity is cast in an unequivocally untenable role. Its secondariness in relation to masculinity – which, in light of its subsequent elaboration, we can see adumbrated in the 'Dora' case[1] – is both temporal and logical. In so far as women ever obtain it or reach it, femininity is not only something second-best, but also a direct substitute for an unattainable masculine ideal. The only vestiges of something which might once have been a woman are buried deep down, in the ancient world that has no communication with the present – lost from the past, impossible to recover, or uncover, in the future.

Both poles appear unappealing in their representations of female subjectivity. In one case, a split that may lead to madness is associated primarily with women; in the second, later version, womanliness has simply ceased to be, ruled out a priori by the surrounding conditions and terms of its (non-) existence. Things seem to go from bad to worse, or from worse to the worst, the pits. But if we dig a little deeper or explore a little more widely, the story of femininity in Freud may turn out to be less straightforward, less of a simple linear movement from pole to pole, than this crude account would suggest. For in one text which lies between these two periods, though nearer the first (it was published in 1907), we find an image of femininity which seems a long way from either of these disheartening pictures.

In 'Delusions and Dreams in Jensen's *Gradiva*', Freud's study of Wilhelm Jensen's novella, it is the girl[2] who seems to have it all, while the man is the one who is deluded, divided and in need of help. Not only that: this is one Freudian text in which everything seems to work out fine. The man doesn't know what he wants, the woman shows him (it's her), and that is the end of it. Gradiva, alias Zoe Bertgang, is congratulated by Freud for her brilliant success, which he calls a 'triumph', no less, comparing her insights and her therapeutic skills with those of the new technique of psychoanalysis.[3] The woman in this text is not passively rooted in one spot, but the active one who understands the situation and takes steps to change it; she lives and loves to the full and her thinking is not represented in the way that masculine speculations are, as something which takes the place of erotic feelings. As though in mockery of the forms of masculine fantasy, the feminine ghost that Norbert thinks he sees turns out to be no ghost, but something more (or less): a down-to-earth living woman who wants to get away from the deathly monumentality of her identification by him as a timeless aesthetic ideal.

But perhaps we should not move so fast. For what if the impression that here Freud is offering a different version of femininity were itself just some feminist delusion brought on, like Norbert Hanold's vision of Zoe as Gradiva, by the heat of the day, the exotic Italian atmosphere Freud evokes from Jensen's story? The possibility that this might be too optimistic an interpretation is reinforced by the fact that there has also been a tendency to consider the work as a kind of playful interlude on Freud's own part, picking up on his evident attraction to a story dealing with someone who shared his own fascination for the archaeological explorations that were taking place at the time on the sites of the ancient world. In this reading, Freud may have been carried away by his personal predilections, but his study remains at the level of a frivolous *divertissement*, in no way presenting itself as a serious alternative to the seriously sombre versions of femininity he elaborates elsewhere.

The identification with the figure of Norbert Hanold takes some quite literal turns in Freud's own biography: he too visited the ruins of Pompeii in the year he read the novella; later, having himself seen the statue of Gradiva in the Vatican Museum in Rome, he acquired a plaster-cast of it which was placed in his consulting-room in Vienna – a practice copied, with further copies of the statue, by Freud's analytical follow-ers of the period.[4] There is certainly no reason to assume that all these Gradivas – in Jensen's text, in Freud's, in the consult-ing rooms of analysts – are identical in their significance, though they surely testify to a widespread masculine fascina-tion with her image, or to a wish to copy the father figure's object of desire. The multiplicity of contemporary Gradivas suggests that the statue's status as a unique object in a single place, from another time, has already suffered some modifica-tions; and as we shall see, Freud's study has much to say about the division that supposedly separates the genuine from the copy or the fake, and the relation of this to the identity of a woman. And perhaps we should not be too hasty either in assuming that the holiday mood is automatically to be rejected as worthless. For this is a text which also puts in question the priorities of the serious and the frivolous, and again in relation to what it identifies as masculine conceptions of the distinction between (serious) work and the aimless pleasures of love and vacation. There may be no one Gradiva, this and not that, because the text refuses and confuses such ready demarcations of two-term hierarchical value.

Sarah Kofman's reading of the Freud study implicitly raises the question of *Gradiva*'s multiple meanings. She is interested in the implications of Freud's own résumé of *Gradiva*, which like any such exercise is selective, cutting out to the same extent that it chooses, but which also – in that he begins to interpolate commentary from the start, and because in effect the résumé is given twice, once as such and then again in the part that is ostensibly that of the interpretation of the now-completed summary – shows up in particularly sharp relief the way that any summary must also be setting itself up as an addition, something to complete a text which must be shown to stand in need of what the commentary now comes to supply.[5] The same, as Kofman suggests, applies to readings of Freud's own text on Jensen's: one interpretation always necessarily leaves out, and implicitly makes way for, another.

Except by a gesture at the end of her study towards the possibilities left unexplored and thus open by the ending of Freud's, when he suddenly throws out an enigmatic allusion to the alternation between sadistic and masochistic tendencies which Norbert evinces, Kofman, the future author of *The Enigma of Woman: Femininity in Freud's Texts*,[6] does not approach anything which might have to do with issues of sexual difference. This is not a reproach, since it is part of her own argument that there is no such thing as a complete or final reading, and no a priori way of privileging one line of interpretation or supplementing over another. By the same token, in looking at the ways that this text distributes the lines of sexual difference and desire, we will find that there is no way that it can be clearly separated from the other themes and questions. And it is here that the strongest case lies for there being something about Freud's Gradiva that makes her different from the other women who make their distinctive appearances or apparitions in his texts.

Near the beginning, when Freud is taking his distance from the interpretations that an evidently unappealing character called 'the psychiatrist' would be likely to bring to Norbert Hanold's case, he declares:

A psychiatrist would perhaps place Norbert Hanold's delusion in the great group of 'paranoia' and possibly describe it as 'fetishistic erotomania', because the most striking thing about it was his being in love with the piece of sculpture and because in the psychiatrist's view, with its tendency to coarsen everything (*seiner alles vergröbernden Affassung*), the young archaeologist's interest in feet and the postures of feet would be bound to suggest 'fetishism'.

(70; 122)

Of course it would never occur to the author of *The Interpretation of Dreams* to participate in such crudely coarsening readings of refined aesthetic activities; but leaving that to one side, what is striking here is that Strachey's translation omits two crucial words, *weiblicher Personen*, between the feet and the (non-) fetishism. For Freud, and in the novella, the interest that Norbert shows is not just for any chance feet, but for quite special feet: the feet of 'female persons'. The fetishism which will come to be related intimately, in Freud's later writing, to the issue of how the two sexes understand their unsymmetrical difference, is invoked here only in passing, never to return. The female persons mentioned by Freud and scotomised by Strachey do, however, figure prominently in the way that the text organises its meanings: for as we shall see, according to its assumptions, no woman could have got herself into Norbert's position of researching female feet in general because he cannot see that he is in love with one particular girl.

In what follows, I shall to some extent be following – though neither faithfully nor in pursuit – in the footsteps of three recent commentators, a psychoanalyst, an artist, and a literary critic who have focused on the femininity of this text. Like Ernest Jones in this (one) respect, Wladimir Granoff sees *Gradiva* as a pleasant, almost wish-fulfilling pause for Freud the man in terms of his own relation to what would later have to be theorised as the inescapability of the castration complex.[7] And Victor Burgin's photomontage, by its own reversals, points up the way in which the story is told unequivocally from a masculine point of view – from Hanold to Jensen to Freud. In the sense that it is about the achievement of the perfect complementarity imagined in the fantasy of meeting the right girl – the complementarity denounced by Lacan's notorious declaration that in reality 'there is no sexual relationship', Burgin sees the text as being essentially a study of the structure of masculinity.[8] In a parallel way, Mary Jacobus situates Freud's study in the context of a persistent connection between masculine theory and the fitting femininity it constantly seeks, so that 'Zoe herself, no less than Gradiva, is made in the image of Hanold's, Jensen's, and Freud's own desire'.[9]

For *Gradiva* is in one sense the *passante* story come true, but with some interesting twists which make it at the same time the *passante* story in reverse. Instead of being irrevocably marked by a woman in the street who acquires, in retrospect, the immutable stillness and inaccessibility of a statue, the hero of Jensen's novella takes a fancy to a statue which turns out to resemble a woman in the street with whom he then falls in love for real. Yet since this woman is also the hero's childhood sweetheart grown up, a second story emerges according to which the object of love was first buried in the form of a statue to whom is then transferred all the interest previously, and then subsequently once more, reserved for the girl herself.

Jensen's plot involves a young archaeologist, one Norbert Hanold, who finds himself taking an excessive interest in the sculpture of a young woman with a highly distinctive turn of foot: Gradiva's 'gait', as Strachey is obliged, for want of another walking word, to translate the much less archaic-sounding *Gangart*, is characterised by the raising of the heel so high that it is almost perpendicular to the ground. Though he does not realise it himself, Norbert is interested because the sculpture is an exact likeness of his childhood sweetheart who lives down the street, one Zoe Bertgang. The new-found passion for this particular object takes him away from his ancient studies far enough for him to ask himself the question whether the statue's idiosyncratic walk corresponds to anything in real life, and to begin looking around him at living, contemporary specimens of women walking in the street. There is one woman who makes an impression on him when he glimpses her from his window, and yes, it is Zoe but at this point he doesn't recognise her. When Zoe's father takes her, and his obsession with the statue takes him, to Pompeii, she, both in love with him herself and able immediately to grasp his more complex situation – a love for her diverted into scholarly researches and half manifesting itself now in the fascination with the statue – succeeds in drawing him out of his delusion, bringing him back to a reality which consists in a perfect mutual love. Ergo, the *passante* – who is also some kind of model *flâneuse*, with her high heel and her sureness of purpose, method and desire – turns out in this case really to be the one and only, to the point where she herself comes back to show the hero that this is so: to bring him out of the fantasy of imagining her as something dead, unattainable, belonging to a past life, and reveal that she stands for the possibility of love and life in the here and now.

But Freud's text on Jensen's is not presented as being about femininity, or masculinity, or love. The title points to the issue of 'Dreams and Delusions', and the preamble – interesting for other reasons, to which we shall return – situates it as a test case for both the psychoanalytic theory of dreams as representing the fulfilment of wishes (Freud's *magnum opus* to date, to which the author of 'Dreams and Delusions' pays due homage by alluding to 'the author of *The Interpretation of Dreams*', had been published in 1900), and the validity of literary evidence for the testing of psychoanalytical hypotheses. It is in this context of the relation of psychoanalysis and creative writing that the text has most often been placed (the Pelican Freud Library, for instance, puts it in the volume on 'Art and Literature').

In its deployment of archaeology as both theme and metaphor, *Gradiva* accords wonderfully with Freud's own predilections – and no very subtle theory of overdetermination is required to show what drew him to the text in addition to its convenient inclusion of three dreams susceptible, in their clear relation to the surrounding events and the characters' preoccupations, to comparison with the psychoanalytic account of the motivation of dreams.[10] Not only is Norbert Hanold an archaeologist by profession, but also most of the action takes place in Pompeii, the city whose ruins were miraculously preserved after the eruption of Vesuvius in AD 79. But the deployment of archaeology is more than a matter of merely anecdotal interest. By another sort of overdetermination, or nether-determination, the archaeological motif is connected via all kinds of passages, both subterranean and superficial, to the interrelated concerns of the book which we will be exploring here: the process of the cure as a kind of excavation; two-level models of surface and depth; scientific knowledge and everyday knowledge; and the status and role of the woman.

Pompeii gave Freud a perfect analogy for the condition of repressed wishes, at once buried and alive, at once past and done and actively impinging upon the present. He was to use it again in his writing; here, he develops the comparison to include a process of excavation equivalent to the technique of analysis in uncovering what is repressed:

> There is, in fact, no better analogy for repression, by which something in the mind is at once made inaccessible and preserved, than burial of the sort to which Pompeii fell a victim and from which it could emerge once more through the work of spades.
>
> (65)

The analysis, like the dig, must laboriously pick away by retracing the stages, going over the same ground as the process by which the repression initially came about. Within Jensen's text, and this is one element on which Freud gleefully pounces, 'digging up' is employed as the metaphor for Zoe's work in getting at the lover she knows is there beneath the mask of scholarly indifference, and also for her own interest in finding something of interest while she is in Pompeii. It turns out to be Norbert, the man and the problem, though she veils it here with her customary knowing denial: 'I told myself I should dig out something interesting here even by myself. Of course I hadn't counted on making the find that I have – I mean my luck in meeting you, Gisa' (53).[11]

The structure, as well as the precise analogy, is a familiar one in Freud. Two times or modes – past and present, wish and reality – are represented topographically in their separation from each other. The task of analysis in its retracing of the steps, its following through the same process as the one that enforced the split, is to make the two relatively compatible with and accessible to one another, thus putting an end to the interferences periodically caused by the futile but unstoppable efforts of the buried repressed wishes to make their way to the surface of actuality.

In the text on *Gradiva*, the archaeological analogy is itself repeatedly employed through the metaphor of digging, but there is also a more general imagery of surface and depth for the representation of hidden or unacknowledged feelings. In a particularly forceful example, less so in the English which turns a formal third-person 'It befell the author' into a simple 'I', there is the following competition for the prestige of priority:

When, from the year 1893 onwards, I plunged into [*er vertiefte*] investigations such as those of mental disturbances, it would certainly never have occurred to me to look for a confirmation of my findings in imaginative writings. I was thus more than a little surprised to find that the author of *Gradiva*, which was published in 1903, had taken as the basis of its creation [*seiner Schöpfung das nämliche zugrunde lege*] the very thing that I believed myself to have freshly discovered [*als neu zu schöpfen*] from the sources of my medical experience.

(79)

What the English version does not bring out here is the directness of the parallel. Both creative writer and psychoanalyst are creators (*schöpfen* and *Schöpfung* corresponding as verb and noun equivalents), and both are diggers down to their sources or ground, from which they take the buried treasure of fresh creations.

Paradoxically, the old and the new appear to be interchangeable here: the would-be 'new' creation is taken from the depths, by burrowing down to dig out something there all the time. This reversibility in the line of scientific discoveries is linked to another, suggested by the consumer connotations of Freud's 'as new'. The expression highlights another two-layer divide which cuts across the whole of this text, and comes to the surface most visibly when he is describing Norbert Hanold's bad bargain at the hotel where, it turns out, Gradiva-Zoe and her father are staying. Having gone in there simply to get some mineral water, he comes out with a much more expensive purchase, ostensibly the clasp taken from the pair of lovers embracing whose bodies were found among the ruins of Pompeii, but actually a fake. In this case, by the exceptional logic which applies to items of cultural value, what is offered 'as old' is worthless because it is new. In the commoner case of fashionable items, the terms are inverted, and newness is the positive criterion.[12]

While the immediate point of this incident as Freud retells it is to demonstrate the psychological realism of Norbert's credulous state at this point when his resistances to erotic feelings are beginning to loosen, the passage draws upon an oppostion between the genuine article and its substitute, between what is *echt* and what is *ersatz*, that occurs in other connections as well: in particular, in relation to Zoe herself. The statue is represented as a copy, even as it is also apparently a perfect physical likeness, 'from the life'; the happy ending of the story will derive from the abandonment of the substitute – or, as a later psychoanalytical vocabulary would have it, of the transitional object – in favour of the real woman for whom Norbert is destined, and whom, when both were children, he originally loved. In this case, what is most authentic – the 'fresh' term – is precisely not the version deep down and buried, except in so far as the childhood time with Zoe is the forgotten memory to which Norbert regains access and which he takes as a measure of Zoe's present worth and desirability. Rather, the modern girl steps out and away from the lower depths to which the statue must now be definitively relegated, well away from the action. The habitual order of priority – the 'buried' layer secretly lingering in its live potential below the surface of the present – has been turned around, for the present proves to be wholly self-sufficient, with no residue of something intractably unassimilable to threaten a subterranean eruption in the future.[13]

But the most serious corollary that is made to the substitute original pairing occurs when Freud moves into comparing the true love of a Zoe–Norbert couple with the interim and secondary love of patient for analyst. Zoe has throughout been granted the status of a doctor, and represented as taking this on herself, as a part she is playing for pragmatic reasons, to secure her end: his cure, which will coincide with his recognition of his love for her. Freud speaks of her 'therapeutic intentions' (53) or her 'psychical treatment' (62), and shows how, just as with the practice that psychoanalysis has recently introduced, she is able to move Norbert nearer to an understanding of his state of mind by a special conversational technique: in her case, the use of deliberately ambiguous phrases that manage to pander to his delusion (that she is a ghost returned from the Pompeii of two thousand years ago) and also to speak accurately of the here and now. Not only may Zoe's methods bear comparison with actual therapy, but also therapy may find itself regarding the fictional Zoe as a source of new insights:

Even the serious treatment [*die ernsthafte Behandlung*] of a real case of illness of the kind could proceed in no other way than to begin by taking up the same ground as the delusional structure and then investigating it as completely as possible. If Zoe was the right person for the job, we shall soon learn, no doubt, how to cure a delusion like our hero's.

(47; 103)

'The emergence of Zoe as a physician' (110) is a theme of enough weight for this phrase to introduce the final chapter of the study. Freud goes much further, in fact, than mere comparison: what shines through his descriptions of Zoe's therapeutic skills is an admiration as for some goddess possessed unfailingly of all the powers to which the supplicant can himself only aspire from a distance. Healing becomes a mysterious art when Zoe's work is described as 'to entice . . . secret knowledge' (93). But there is nothing magical in this for Zoe herself. Freud falls over himself in praise of her 'lucid clarity [of mind]' *'die hellste Geistesklarheit'*, and speaks – in an address that takes up the image of the divine warrior Mars Gradivus conjured up under the feminine name – of her 'triumph of ingenuity and wit to be able to express the delusion and the truth in the same words' (107).

Zoe produces *double entendres* deliberately to match her understanding of her patient's unconscious inclinations. Responding to Norbert's words and behaviour as meaning something other than they seem, she does not challenge him head-on or heart-on, but leads him to realise for himself the hidden feelings he has and she divines. And in her interpretation of his behaviour as a cover for the genuine, buried sense of the second layer, Zoe has some further female allies. These are the women in the street who, when Norbert goes about conducting what, picking up Jensen's own phrase, Freud calls his 'pedestrian researches' (82; 132)[14] to determine whether Gradiva's gait is realistic or not:

> The women and girls in the street, whom he chose as the subjects of his investigation, must, of course, have taken another, crudely erotic view of his behaviour, and we cannot but think them right.

(75; 127)[15]

Women in general, as well as Zoe in particular, are given full marks for spotting what a real doctor would judge to be the correct reading of Norbert's behaviour. The two-tier model of masculine subjectivity comes naturally to them: beneath a scholarly question lies an erotic wish. Born therapists, they are not themselves in need of analysis, since there is nothing to analyse. Their own thoughts and desires are implicitly like Zoe's, all of an untorn piece, up front and known to themselves. The analogy between Zoe's dealings with her would-be lover and a therapist's with a patient leads Freud, as he draws to the end of his study, to ask the disquieting question about the relative efficacy of love and analysis as therapeutic methods. Zoe's *Liebesheilung*, her 'cure by love' (113; 158), corresponds exactly to the procedure of analytic therapy, in which a liberated capacity for loving always takes the physician as its object. But more than this, Zoe's own love for Norbert in this case means that her situation and her success are in fact superior to those of an ordinary cure:

> It is here that the differences begin, which make the case of Gradiva an ideal one which medical technique cannot attain. Gradiva was able to return the love which was making its way from the unconscious into consciousness, but the doctor cannot. Gradiva had herself been the object of the earlier, repressed love; her figure at once offered the liberated current of love a desirable aim. The doctor has been a stranger, and must endeavour to become a stranger once more after the cure; he is often at a loss what advice to give the patients he has cured as to how in real life [*im Leben*] they can use their recovered capacity to love. To indicate the expedients and substitutes of which the doctor therefore makes use to help him to approximate with more or less success to the model [*dem Vorbild*] of a cure by love which has been shown to us by our author – all this would take us much too far away from the task before us.
>
> (113; 159)

The word 'ideal' here is repeated from an earlier reference to Zoe's 'ideal position' (112): the status of this instance as a 'model' that can only be imitated, never replicated, in the normal conditions of analysis, makes it into something like a Platonic form. But there is a paradox here, for it is precisely in that her love, unlike the love that appears in an ordinary therapeutic cure, has its proper place in real life and not in the therapeutic setting, that Zoe's situation is different. In comparison with ordinary cases, she represents both an inaccessible ideal or model, and something closer to life than they are.

But Zoe's idiosyncratic personifications may also suggest a different way of understanding Freud's impasse in thinking about the difference between the two types of cure by love, the real and the artificial. Norbert Hanold's problem is that he is sunk so far into his archaeological depths that he has lost sight completely of the life around him: in both time and place, he is somewhere else. The Gradiva statue figures as a first inching out of the past, because it strikes Norbert himself as being not altogether ancient: as Freud repeats from Jensen, it has something ' "of today" ', *etwas 'heutiges'* (37; 94; also 74; 126). The idiosyncratic foot thus moves Gradiva away from the spot from which she seemed unequivocally to come; indeed, Norbert becomes so unsure of her provenance that his speculations transport her in rapid succession from Rome to Greece and thence to Pompeii at the time of the eruption, which will become the unacknowledged motive, buried like the city itself, for his impromptu journey to Italy.

But if we look twice at the opposite images of Gradiva-Zoe, the model Greek statue and the modern urban girl, something else now appears that previously passed without notice, as part of the linguistic scenery. Zoe's look 'of today' is placed in quotation marks, as though to indicate a doubt about the obviousness of the here and now. Far from being as immediately recognisable as it might seem at first sight, the look 'of today' is just that, a look, a citation of something whose reality is no more present than the past; and the order of priority which up till 'now' has seemed so clearly to distinguish the life from the reproduction or the model from the copy, suddenly shows up as much less certain. As with what English calls, in a strikingly uncertain pleonasm, 'real' life, it now looks as though the look of today is just as much of a second-order representation as the ancient icon. This then puts a different aspect on the hypothetical differentiation between real love and the 'love' of the analytic setting.

Zoe's 'mockery' (*Spott*) is frequently mentioned, by Jensen and then by Freud. As with her skill in reading Norbert, it is a trait she shares with people in the street, who make fun of him when he rushes out early one morning clad only in a dressing gown, thinking he has seen his Gradiva. But with Zoe, the mockery is affectionately playful, not the collective unkindness of an anonymous crowd, and the fact that her laughter at him conceals no nastiness – no ulterior motive – itself becomes something which Norbert has to establish, and which distinguishes her own easy-going attitude to life from his. As in a comic-strip bubble, we are given the future suitor's thoughts verbatim – and this is Freud's imagination, not one of his citations from Jensen:

> And now let us make a bold attempt at replacing Hanold's 'remarkably senseless' dream by the unconscious thoughts that lay behind it and were as unlike it as possible. They ran, perhaps, as follows: 'She is staying in the "Sun" with her father. Why is she playing this game with me [*warum spielt sie solches Spiel mit mir*]? Does she want to make fun of me [*ihren Spott mit mir treiben*]? Or can it possibly be that she loves me and wants to have me as her husband?'
>
> (105; 152)

In fact, her 'Spiel' is just what makes her so successful an analyst: she leads him a dance in which she is unequivocally in control, calling the steps and knowing the full situation when he is only aware of one side of it (such that the reader's identification is with her and not with Norbert). This means that her actions can be ironic (her initial play on the 'sun' uses Norbert's delusion about Gradiva being a mid-day ghost in tandem with the name of the 'Hotel del Sole', where she, Zoe, really is), implying a strategic disentanglement and deployment of the elements she sees as constituting his division of mind. She knows what she wants and what he wants; her doubling is a matter of putting one and one together, unifying the strands set apart in him, in such a way that he is not abruptly confronted with a challenge to his delusion but is able to come to a recognition of the real state of things for himself.

This begins with her own image, divided between the statue and the living woman, between death and life (the literal meaning of her name, Zoe, reinforces this further), between a ghost and the girl next door. The love between her and Norbert is so close to home, in fact, that it verges on staying within the family. For one thing, the two have known each other since they were children, and it is the priority of this long-founded love which is taken as the justification for its continuity and genuineness: it is a return to the origin as pure source – though it's a suitably polymorphous kind of purity that includes some 'knufften und pnufften' – 'bumping and thumping' in Strachey's equally playful rendering (56; 110). In the Freudian account that was not yet fully developed at the time when the Gradiva study was written, first loves are certainly the strongest, but they are also the ones that have to be given up in order for the child to go out into the world. In Gradiva, it is as if there need be no boundary: Norbert and Zoe are like brother and sister to one another, and this past means not that their union is henceforth ruled out, but on the contrary that they are perfectly matched for a future together.

Only one element of their respective parental backgrounds is mentioned by Freud. Where Jensen lays some emphasis on Norbert's choice of archaeology in relation to his father, Freud leaves out all reference to this side. For him, as in Zoe's reading, Norbert's penchant for archaeology is a straightforward substitute for love. For Zoe herself, love is always love and Norbert is a straightforward substitute for her father:

> Fraülein Zoe, the embodiment of cleverness and clarity (die Verkörperung der Klugheit und Klarheit), makes her own mind quite transparent to us. While it is in any case the general rule for a normally constituted girl to turn her affection towards her father in the first instance, Zoe, who had no one in her family but her father, was especially ready to do so. But her father had nothing left over for her: all his interest was engrossed by the objects of his science. So she was obliged to cast her eyes around upon other people, and became especially attached to her young playmate. When he too ceased to have any eyes for her (keine Aügen mehr für sie hatte), her love was not shaken by it but rather increased, for he had become like her father, was, like him, absorbed by science and held apart by it from life and from Zoe.
>
> (58; 112)

This wonderfully double-edged passage begins with the happy unity of body and intellect in Zoe's perfect transparency to herself and her readers. Then, this paragon of modern femininity turns out to have been born to love in a way that boys, by implication, are not. There is never any doubt that Zoe has to direct her love onto a person, rather than diverting it into archaeology or anything else; it is only a question of finding someone who has enough left over in relation to his own other interests to be able to return it with interest. Freud does not specify that the girl's object of love had to be male; in fact the statement that there was just no-one else apart from her father around at home would seem to suggest this is not a fundamental criterion. He does, however, restrict this psychical story to 'a normally constituted girl', who is a romantic heroine from the start, waiting for the one who will only have eyes for her.

Such a summary of Gradiva's development sounds like an actualisation of the situation that Freud will later determine as a kind of oedipal sedentariness for girls who, once they have found their father as an object of love, have no motive (in the way that the castration complex is for boys) to leave the 'haven' where they are installed. Here, it is put quite straight: Gradiva moves over to her neighbour simply because her father can't give her the love she seeks. It is not a shock which turns her from the parent, but simply that she has to go elsewhere to get what she wants.

Masculine development, implicitly, proceeds along different lines. Without there being any further account of for it, or of the reasons why it applies to him and not to her, Freud explains Norbert's turning away from Zoe as the effect of repression, a concept he then goes on to elaborate for his readers:

> With the young man, things had taken a different turn. Archaeology took hold of him and left him with an interest only in women of marble and bronze. His childhood friend-ship, instead of being strengthened into a passion, was dissolved, and his memories of it passed into such a profound forgetfulness that he did not recognize or notice his early playmate when he met her in society. . . . A forgetting of this kind has been given the name of 'repression' in psy-chopathology . . .
>
> (59)

In fact, a forgetting of this kind is just what has not been given the name of 'repression' in Freud's psychopathology. In the most salient example in his later theories of an early passion that is 'dissolved', the difference is clearly marked: a boy's

Oedipus complex is precisely not repressed, but overcome, so that he is able to leave his mother behind with a clean unconscious and go on to other women, while the girls have trouble getting themselves beyond their first loves. These later developments or stagnations in Freud's thinking help to focus the significance of this passage, which in effect puts both sexes in the position that is subsequently only to be the girl's. Far from being an impediment, this remaining in the same place is represented as a delightfully natural destiny.

In the ultimately harmonious unfolding of this version of affective development, the difference between the sexes amounts to the fact that one suffers repression and gets a divided psyche along the way, and the other doesn't; the one who has remained unaffected can then come to the rescue of the other, restoring him to his original capacities – bringing him back to 'life'. For Zoe's therapy consists in showing Norbert that it is not she but he who has been effectively dead: she chides him at the end for his insistence on ' "someone having to die so as to come alive' " (62). This 'life', by contrast with images of distance and division – the past out of sight of the present, aesthetic models distinct from reality, Greece or Pompeii, ancient and far away instead of Norbert's home town – is represented as the modernity from which Norbert's ancient preoccupations have withdrawn him. Zoe's abandonment of what she calls her 'underworld role' (106; 152) is a return to the present day, and to her ordinary self rather than a mythical part taken up alongside it. But this does not imply that Zoe stands or steps for the simplicity of the unequivocal or the simple-minded. For as we have seen, the 'today' in which she prefers to take her place is already double, or at least not clearly one, marking itself with an ironic possibility of distance even as it names the immediacy of the here and now. Gradiva does not transport her man from a simple past to an equally simple present, but instead to a world in which the differences are less sharply divided.

Gradiva's modern look breaks her aesthetic completeness as a work of art removed from present times and present concerns. She appears now as something like a literal manifestation of Baudelaire's insistence in *The Painter of Modern Life* that art is always modern as well as eternal; and that the modern is 'fleeting', on the move, where the timeless remains statically in its place. Her two aspects, as ancient statue and twentieth-century girl,[16] bring into sharp relief the disjunction for Norbert between a consoling past and an uninteresting present unconnected with it; between objects of aesthetic admiration and objects of erotic desire; between authentic and trivial pursuits.

This superimposition of ancient and modern aspects is repeated in the plot device of the novella which takes Norbert and Zoe to Pompeii. Here Norbert is actually on the site of the classical past to which he has been so thoroughly attached; but at the same time, the city is now, in the modern world, a tourist attraction, complete with hotels, mineral water and souvenirs. The modernity that Norbert finds through his search for Gradiva's living counterpart is not just not past, but positively up-to-date: a world of travel and cities, as well as of youthful amorous pleasures. What is old has taken on the special value which marks it off as 'old': a Pompeii unearthed from its burial to become something worth looking at within the world of 'today'.

The celebration of Zoe as the bearer of modern 'life' is linked in turn to another marked term of Freud's text, which is the notion of the everyday. Like the notion of 'today', the everyday is revealing because of its wayward, unpredictable deployment, moving between two principal senses: the everyday is what is considered ordinary or unremarkable, and it is also something differentiated from scholarship and science, the preoccupations of Norbert and of Zoe's father. Both these senses are combined in the discussion of the validity of creative writing as evidence for the psychoanalytic theory of dreams which forms part of Freud's preamble, where forces are clearly ranged according to two heterogeneous sides:

> Now in this dispute as to the estimation in which dreams should be held, imaginative writers seem to be on the same side as the ancients, as the superstitious public [das aberglaübische Volk] and as the author of The Interpretation of Dreams. For when an author makes the characters constructed by his imagination dream, he follows the everyday experience [der alltäglischen Erfahrung], that people's thoughts and feelings are continued in sleep and he aims at nothing else than to depict his heroes' states of mind by their dreams.

But creative writers are valuable allies and their evidence is to be prized highly, for they are apt to know a whole host of things between heaven and earth of which our philosophy has not let us dream. In their knowledge of the mind they are far in advance of us everyday people [*uns Alltagsmenschen*] for they draw upon sources which we have not yet opened up for science.

(34; 90)

There is a hesitation here as to where the writer of this passage stands, wavering as he does between his prestigious third-person position and his identification as one of 'us', the first knowing more than the scientists and the second less than creative writers. But what is interesting for our purposes is that the significance of 'everyday experience' is not perceived by the 'everyday people' who are scientists. In this prospect of future scientific conquest ('not yet'), an advance of knowledge through time, the everyday, as both the most ancient and the most modern of philosophical dreams, has not yet come into its own.

Later, the importance of everyday experience is underlined through examples. Having analysed Norbert's unconsciousness of the real reason for his journey to Italy (to find Gradiva), Freud continues:

This is certainly taken from the life [*dem Leben abgelauscht*]. One does not need to be suffering from a delusion in order to behave like this. On the contrary, it is an event of daily occurence [*ein alltägliches Vorkommis*] for a person – even a healthy person – to deceive himself over the motives for an action and to become conscious of them only after the event [*nachträglich*], provided only that a conflict between several currents of feeling furnishes the necessary conditions of such a confusion.

(89–90; 139)

Everyday knowledge here is a crazy knowledge, everyday both in that it is small-scale (anyone can be mad this way), and in that it repeats itself. (This is also, as it happens, one of Freud's earlier descriptions of the effect of *Nachträglichkeit* or 'deferred action', most fully elaborated in the 'Wolf Man' case history (1919), whereby the past is not given once and for all, in a simple chronological sequence, but is subject to modification by a retrospective look back from the here and now.)

The theme of the everyday appears once more in the course of a third general statement, again in the context of an imaginary defence of the pertinence of creative writing to the study of pathology:

> [T]he frontier between states of mind described as normal and pathological is in part a conventional one and in part so fluctuating [so fliessende] that each of us probably crosses it many times in the course of a day.
>
> (68–9; 121)

Here, everyday life is implicitly something unconventional, not subject to the law; it is also a region that is indeterminately situated between, on both sides of, sanity and madness: neither one nor the other, but forever re-establishing or abolishing their difference across the vague line that is never fixed once and for all. It is also, like the Zoe who walks in her difference from the statue of Gradiva, a condition of movement.

Freud's text itself oscillates to and fro between an insistence upon strict demarcations and a looser enjoyment of their absence. He had himself brought forward the significance of the quotidian (in The Psychopathology of Everyday Life, published just two years before the Gradiva study), as well as in the way that the new therapeutic technique positively encouraged the inclusion of supposedly irrelevant bits and pieces of daily life. But at the same time, this fluidity – the 'fluctuating' line – is periodically dealt with as something in need of constraint and definitive ordering.

There could hardly be a more categorical statement than this, towards the end:

> Our procedure consists in the conscious observation of abnormal mental processes in other people so as to be able to elicit and announce their laws.
>
> (115)

Or again, right at the start, when he is laying out the aims of the reading of Gradiva in terms of its potential usefulness to the development of knowledge about dreams and creative writing, Freud puts it like this:

There is far less freedom and arbitrariness [Willkür] in
mental life, however, than we are inclined to assume – there
may even be none at all. What we call chance in the world
outside can, as is well known, be resolved into laws [Gesetze].
So, too, what we call arbitrariness in the mind rests upon
laws, which we are only now beginning dimly to suspect.

(35; 91)

Here, the 'more things in heaven and earth' have taken on a
more sombre tone than in the earlier passage: these truths that
writers and ordinary people glimpse turn out to be future
'laws', and take on the hard not fast fixity of a monumental
inflexibility, models beneath the movement of life, a hidden
solid substance rather than the chances of an ever-changing
surface. It is as though when science comes forward to take
over the territory of the everyday, it will suppress the looseness that differentiated it in the first place and made it appear
to be the next step.

This same perpetual swing between the potentially scientific
and the pleasurably mobile, when the latter – in the form of
day-dreams, for instance – is itself the subject-matter brought
in for legislation, can be found in others of Freud's writings of
this period, for the Gradiva text is one of a whole group in which
he is either directly or implicitly looking at questions of fantasy,
day-dreaming and artistic imagination.[17] In the Gradiva study,
one or two laws are indeed promulgated along the way, in
addition to the general declaration of intentions at the beginning. These laws tend, however, to be less in the form of
scientific inferences from the evidence than ready knowledge
which can be used to explain an action in advance. The most
striking instance of this occurs during a discussion of the way
in which what has been repressed re-emerges 'from the field of
the instruments that served to bring about the repression'.
Freud continues:

It was right that an antique, the marble sculpture of a
woman, should have been what tore our archaeologist away
from his retreat from love and warned him to pay off the
debt to life with which we are burdened [belastet] from our
birth.

(74; 126)

Norbert is timely ripped from what is represented as an unacceptable abandonment of love. His return to life and love is not for the pleasure but because that is the law, and it comes in the form of a warning rather than an attractive offer. It is the human condition to come into the world with a debt to pay off, rather than credit to spend: you are born in the red, and clearing your debt to life will presumably free you from this importunate creditor only to restore you to the pre- or non-life place from which you emerged. At any rate – and whatever the rate of exchange – this does not seem a very promising deal, where the 'life' that has elsewhere been represented as Norbert's way out of the isolation of his premature grave now itself takes on so constraining a role, the underworld and underside to the lightness of the life 'of today' that Zoe holds out.

This darker side to Freud's study appears to be continued in other aspects of his conclusions. Following one of his commonest rhetorical strategies, he raises a possible objection which is attributed to a particular class of readers (frequently philosophers), and then squashes it with the reply from psychoanalysis. But in this instance, the situation is doubly complicated: the objection to which he alludes is itself an objection to another hypothetical reading:

> [T]he author, no doubt to the satisfaction of his female readers [gewiss zur Befriedigung seiner Leserinnen], arranged that his story, a not uninteresting one otherwise, should have the usual happy ending in marriage. It would have been more consistent and equally possible, the argument will proceed, if the young scientist, after his error had been pointed out, had taken his leave of the young lady with polite thanks and given as the reason for refusing her love the fact that he was able to feel an intense interest in antique women made of bronze or marble, and in their originals [Urbilder] if they were accessible to contact, but that he did not know what to do with contemporary girls of flesh and blood. The author, in short, had quite arbitrarily [willkürlich] tacked a love story on to his archaeological phantasy.

(110; 155)

As with the women in the street, the supposed women readers will in fact turn out to be vindicated against the sceptics, for their natural satisfaction proceeds according to the observation of the laws of mental life which the creative writer, with an equivalent intuitive understanding, has drawn out. But if female readers of Freud's text are inclined to be satisfied with this flattering representation of their satisfactions as scientifically validated, they may find their pleasure somewhat abruptly curtailed by the expansion which follows. In Norbert's case, the 'repressed erotic desire' which must be seen not as an arbitrary frill but as psychologically accurate takes the form (as our author does not fail to remind us) of 'his curiosity about her "bodily nature", his jealousy, and his brutal masculine instinct for mastery [der brutale männliche Bemächtungstrieb]' (111; 156)

This may be a happy ending for masculinity, but it looks like a brutal turnabout for women. What at first seemed so satisfying a fantasy of a Freudian text in which femininity was something other than a site of madness or a derivative relation to a masculine norm is coming to appear much like another version of the same old story. Love may triumph, but only where there is a clear division betwen masculine and feminine dispositions there from the beginning, and only with laws of psychical development which seem, in a literally 'conventional' way, to make love the be-all and end-all of a woman's life where for men it occupies a different place.

But all is not lost. In so far as this is a text written before the hard lines of sexual differentiation according to the law of the castration complex has been set in place in Freud's thinking, we may perhaps be entitled to look upon it not so much, or not only, as a typical male fantasy of femininity (that would be to repeat the same gesture of sexual normalisation which comes as such a disappointment when it emerges in Freud), but also as an exploration whose difference is to be sought in the openness which throughout seems to triumph rhetorically over the moments of legalistic firmness. And this openness emanates from the girl whose brightness, in every sense, shines through, from her supposed appearance as a 'mid-day ghost' to her lively mockery of her over-scholarly friend. We might also take heart from a figure who appears in Norbert's third dream as 'the enigmatic 'lady colleague' [der rätselhaften "Kollegin"]' (97; 145). She is later identified with Zoe's honeymooning friend Gisela, but she is also, implicitly, Zoe herself in her equivocal role on the one hand as a peer for both her father and her lover (all three occupy themselves with digging things up), and on the other as the intellectual and therapeutic match for the psychoanalyst, whose work she performs to perfection.

For Zoe does more than simply slot in to her allotted happy ending: she suggests a variation. Although Freud makes the connection, as we have seen, Zoe herself does not wish to identify the two men in her life for long. Her image of Norbert as an 'archaeopteryx' fuses him and her father – both linguistically and in its meaning – bringing together their archaeological and entomological interests in a single extinct fossil. But with her customary lucidity, Zoe herself diagnoses this assimilation as being undesirable, urging her lover not to become like her father (this is the only point at which her mockery is said to be 'bitter'): he must not 'keep too closely to the model on which she had chosen him' (64). In other words, he should not assume that she is suffering from his former affliction, measuring the object of love by an immutable standard to which it could never conform, holding her apart in the form of a lifeless image which makes her unrecognisable in reality. The original is not to be sought or emulated in vain, and in a world 'of today', the pure ideal is necessarily a thing of the past.

And in spite of the separation of masculine from feminine roles – or 'duties' – in lovemaking, the story (both Freud's and Jensen's) has undermined this all along. It is Zoe, after all, who takes the initiative: like Orpheus, she goes down to the underworld to rescue the one she loves, steps out to get what she wants. More than this, it is from her feminine place of knowledge that Gradiva-Zoe is able to adopt her double role as ghost and girl next door, aesthetically ideal woman and sisterly friend. Her mockery enables her to make use of the two positions for her own ends, rather than being confined into one or other of them. She is in effect a past and present mistress at sending back a masculine double standard where it came from, so that the marble lady vanishes in favour of the much more savvy figure of the modern girl who does not stand either for conformity or for rebellion from the 'laws' of masculine minds, but instead is able to walk all over them, treating them (in both senses) with the irony of 'today'.

NOTES

1 See chapter 8 in this volume, p. 140.
2 Not just the girl, but 'la girl' herself, in French descriptions of this text. See the Introduction by J.-B. Pontalis to the French translation of Freud's and Jensen's texts (Paris: Gallimard, 1986), pp. 19–20, where he refers to the incontestable relevance for the Gradiva case of the symbolic equation of 'Girl = phallus' posited by Fenichel and taken up again by Lacan.
3 Freud, 'Delusions and dreams in Jensen's Gradiva' (1907), PFL, vol 14, p. 107. Further references will be given within the main text.
4 See Lydia Flem, La vie quotidienne des patientes de Freud à Vienne (Paris: Hachette, 1990).
5 See Sarah Kofman, Quatre romans analytiques (Paris: Galilée, 1973), trans. Sarah Wykes, Freud and Fiction (Cambridge: Polity, 1991).
6 Sarah Kofman, L'Enigme de la femme: La femme dans les textes de Freud (Paris: Galilée, 1982), trans. Catherine Porter (Ithaca: Cornell University Press, 1985).
7 Wladimir Granoff, 'Gradiva entre les colonnes', in La pensée et le féminin (Paris: Minuit, 1976), pp. 381–403.
8 Victor Burgin, Between (Oxford: Basil Blackwell and the Institute for Contemporary Arts, 1986); Lacan, Encore.
9 Mary Jacobus, Reading Woman: Essays in Feminist Criticism, (New York: Columbia University Press, 1986) p. 95.
10 In fact, it was Jung who suggested the book to Freud – an event to which Freud alludes near the beginning of the text (p. 35).
11 'Ich sagte mir, irgend etwas Interessantes würde ich wohl schon allein hier ausgraben. Freilich, auf den Fund, den ich gemacht – ich meine das Glück, dich zu treffen, Gisa, hatte ich mit keinem Gedanken gerechnet.' Wilhelm Jensen, Gradiva: Ein pompejanisches Phantasiestück (1903), reprinted with Freud's text on the novella (Frankfurt am Main: Fischer Taschenbuch Verlag, 1973), p.75. Further citations are included within the text, following the reference to the English translation.
12 Contemporary art, as opposed to established art, lies directly on the faultline between the values of fashion and the value of art as situated by definition outside the fluctuations of the tastes of the moment. So it seems fitting that when in 1937 André Breton and his colleagues opened an art gallery in Paris to show and sell new works by surrealist artists, they called it Gradiva. (It was not a commercial success and folded within the year.)
13 Jensen makes the link, and Freud and his commentators have repeated it, between the name Gradiva and the god of war, Mars Gradivus, which gives Zoe's statuesque equivalent a name which is not only a masculine but also aggressive. The unfolding of the action in the vicinity of a volcano further reinforces this, by suggesting the weapon-forging god Vulcan.
14 The same phrase occurs later (p. 91), but the German quotation it translates is slightly different: pedestrischen Untersuchungen rather than

pedestrischen Prüfungen.

15 Like many of the topics in Freud's text, this one is repeated from an earlier appearance, where the women's reactions are described asmore interested, less detached and comparable to the doctor than here:

> Now however, the scientific task which he had taken on compelled him, in dry, but more especially in wet, weather, to look eagerly in the street at women's and girl's feet as they came into view – an activity which brought him some angry, and some encouraging, glances from those who came under his observation.

(38)

16 Just: Jensen's novella was published in 1903, a fact on which Freud lays considerable emphasis when he takes it upon himself to argue for the independence of the discoveries made by himself and Breuer in the 1890's from those to be found within Jensen's *Schöpfung* (see p. 165).

17 See for instance 'Creative writers and day-dreaming' (1908), 'Hysterical fantasies and their relation to bisexuality' (1908).

I can't resist adding that in both sets of proofs for this book, Gradiva came out as Gravida on the title page – revealing, perhaps, a pregnant woman buried in the name alongside the warrior Mars Gradivus noticed by Freud and Jensen.

Index